FUTUREFACE

FUTUREFACE

A FAMILY MYSTERY, A SEARCH FOR IDENTITY,
AND THE TRUTH ABOUT BELONGING

ALEX WAGNER

ADAPTED FOR YOUNG READERS

DELACORTE PRESS

All rights reserved. Published in the United States by Delacorte Press,
an imprint of Random House Children's Books, a division of
Penguin Random House LLC, New York.

This work is based on *Futureface,* copyright © 2018 by Alex Wagner.
Originally published in hardcover in the United States by One World, an imprint of
Random House, a division of Penguin Random House LLC, New York, in 2018.

Delacorte Press is a registered trademark and the colophon
is a trademark of Penguin Random House LLC.

Visit us on the Web! rhcbooks.com

Educators and librarians, for a variety of teaching tools,
visit us at RHTeachersLibrarians.com

Library of Congress Cataloging-in-Publication Data
Names: Wagner, Alex, author.
Title: Futureface : a family mystery, a search for identity, and the
truth about belonging / Alex Wagner.
Description: First edition. | New York : Delacorte Press, an imprint of
Random House Children's Books, a division of Penguin Random House, 2020.
Identifiers: LCCN 2019004810 | ISBN 978-1-9848-9662-9 (hc) |
ISBN 978-1-9848-9663-6 (glb) | ISBN 978-1-9848-9664-3 (ebook)
Subjects: LCSH: Wagner, Alex—Juvenile literature. |
Journalists—United States—Biography—Juvenile literature. |
Women journalists—United States—Biography—Juvenile literature.
Classification: LCC PN4874.W254 A3 2019 | DDC 070.92 [B]—dc23

The text of this book is set in 12-point Bembo MT Pro.

Printed in the United States of America
10 9 8 7 6 5 4 3 2 1
First Edition

For Cy and Rafa, of course

INTRODUCTION

There is a line between Us and Them, and I've seen it. Or at least part of it. Along the Arizona-Mexico border—in the American town of Nogales—is a sky-high, thirty-foot steel fence. Politicians say that border fences like this one are built to keep citizens from separate countries on their own sides of the border. In truth, this fence, built by Americans, is intended to keep Mexicans in Mexico. And to keep America . . . American. Whatever that means.

It's only mildly effective.

Back when I visited the United States–Mexico border, I was the anchor of a cable news show. The border had become an American obsession. Our country was spending billions of dollars to guard it, using agents, drones, cameras, and exotic military hardware. The fence was only one part of this expensive and sometimes violent border patrol—and I went to Nogales, Arizona, to see it up close.

We were taking a break from shooting the news show, when I suddenly noticed a pair of fruit sellers on the Mexican side of the wall. They lassoed a rope to the top of a border fence post, climbed up, and, before I knew it, shimmied down to the American side of the border. All in under five minutes, in broad daylight—with a border patrol guard stationed right there along the barrier.

All of a sudden, in departing from the land of their ancestors, these two fruit sellers were part of a different story. They were crossing a high wall marking an invisible border. They were also crossing a line inside themselves: between the native and the immigrant—one who already belongs and one who has just arrived. They had become something new. They were part of an adventure story that has defined human existence from the beginning of our history—a movement from one land to another.

Stories like this—about immigrants, refugees, exiles, and internal migrants—have always had a hold on me, perhaps because of my own family's history of migrations, escapes, settlement, and assimilation. But these are universal struggles, too.

In 2013, I spent a few months researching Maricopa

County, Arizona, intrigued by the diverse group of inhabitants, people who had been within the United States for varying lengths of time. There were descendants of homesteaders; Latinos whose families had been there for centuries; Native Americans whose families had been there for millennia; and new immigrants who had only just crossed deserts or completed oceans of paperwork to get there from Mexico and Central America. All the striving, all the risks immigrants took to get here, to build a better, safer life for themselves—what did it mean to belong? Just as importantly: Who got to decide? Each answer gave rise to new questions.

In reality, immigration isn't a story of outsiders versus insiders. It's a story about the messy, sad, terrifying, and occasionally beautiful experience of leaving one place and starting over in another. My interest in the subject wasn't simply about the politics, but in immigration as an internal change. What went on inside ourselves when we moved somewhere new and became something new? What went on inside ourselves when we lost one home and made another? Immigration raises into relief some of our most essential questions: *Who am I? Where do I belong?* And in that way, it's deeply tied to an exploration of American identity. Here we are, in a nation of immigrants, exiles, captives, refugees, and displaced natives, asked to answer these soul-searching questions.

They are questions I've asked myself when I thought about my Burmese mother and American father, when I thought about the country that pushed and pulled me in different directions. All this contemplation made me both hungry for identity and tired of obsessing over it. It made me want a simple answer, an easy story about who we are and why we're here together. I started to see my preoccupation with immigrants, exiles, and refugees—and my questions about home and identity and belonging—as the edge of a longer, more complex puzzle. Turns out, the mystery I was really trying to solve was my own.

PART I

SOLITAIRE

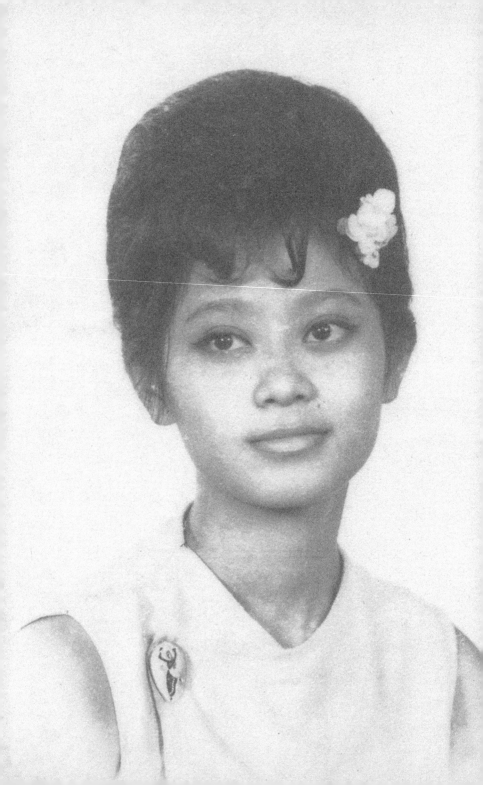

CHAPTER ONE

played a lot of solitaire growing up. I was an only child and a nerd and thus on my own a lot of the time. When I wasn't, I was asked to mind my manners and keep quiet around the adults. For most of my adolescence, I used a weathered pack of dark blue playing cards for those solitaire games. On the back, embossed in gold, was the logo of the International Brotherhood of Teamsters: a pair of horses' heads above a wagon wheel. Shuffling the deck, I felt . . . alone. I was on the outside, wishing to be on the inside—where everyone else seemed to be.

The Teamsters union was where my mother worked in 1971, toward the end of the height of American labor organizing. She had immigrated to America from

Rangoon, Burma,* in 1965, escaping a military dictatorship. From her initial landing pad in Washington, D.C., she went on to attend Swarthmore College, and became passionate about leftist politics.

After college, she found a job at the Teamsters union, a group supporting blue-collar workers' rights. That led to an interview for a job at the Alliance for Labor Action. The man who interviewed her there was my father, and from the moment they met, she couldn't stand him. Perhaps that should have been a warning, but instead it became their meet-cute: They hated each other! And then they got married.

My father's ancestry began on the other side of the world. He was the fourth child of a mail carrier in rural Iowa, the son of an Irish American mother and a father who claimed roots in Luxembourg. My dad showed an early interest in politics and, like my mother, came to Washington to work on liberal causes. He had longish

---

* Burma is now officially known as Myanmar. This dates back to 1989, when a military takeover—installing a government known as the *military junta*—changed the name of the country. The military junta was carrying out violence and human rights violations across the country; it's thought that they changed the country's name to distract from this negative attention. My family—and all the Burmese exiles I have known— continued to call the country Burma, as an act of defiance—a refusal to acknowledge an illegitimate junta. At any rate, throughout this book I refer to the country and its people as Burma and Burmese. Though the name Burma unfortunately also has negative connotations (it stems from the era of British colonialism), it remains the way in which my family has identified itself and separated itself from a regime that has persecuted and killed its own citizens—and continues to.

hair, worked on George McGovern's presidential campaign, and knew the counterculture writer Hunter S. Thompson. My mother's and father's faraway histories intersected on a bridge of early 1970s bohemianism. Only a few generations back, their families had been separated by oceans and mountain ranges and steppes. But in Washington, their shared values were enough to draw them close.

They were married in 1975 and several years later had their only child—me, a daughter born of an unlikely set of Burmese-Luxembourgian-Irish bloodlines. Of this heritage I knew little. Our Burmese story was relayed to me by my mother and grandmother, only occasionally, and almost always over some homemade, traditional dish. A pot of chicken curry would summon some certain memory, which would then spiral into another memory, or into a snippet of family history. But only a snippet. Burma was kept at a distance from our American lives.

On my European side, my great-grandfather (my father's grandfather) left the Old World sometime during the late nineteenth century. I didn't know much about his departure and why he'd made it, or even much about the place where he began: Luxembourg, the sixth smallest country in the world, in a town called Esch. These details weren't much discussed, which gave them an air of mystery.

My father's mother and her family were from Ireland,

but as far as American family histories went, Ireland didn't interest me much. The best parts of being Irish, according to what I knew, had become as familiar as St. Patrick's Day. The cliché was that Irish daughters were redheaded and pale, and the sons would drink and get in fistfights. I was definitely not in either of those categories. So Luxembourg was the ancestral origin I most frequently cited, but that was a little like being from the dark side of the moon, or an island in the center of an ocean. It was like being from somewhere almost no one had heard of.

As a child I didn't think much about these family histories. It didn't cross my mind that I was, in some way, the outcome of all of them combined. And no one told me much about our origins anyway. I was mostly taught that my ancestors, whoever they were—the people in my family tree, by the random genetic alignments in the universe—should in no way affect my destiny. Anyway, wasn't that the whole point of America? Dynasties were for the Old World. Tradition was something held aloft by queens and kings, and bloodlines were for horses and pharaohs.

Here, in the United States, we could be whoever we wanted to be instead. This country, as we had been taught, was about moving forward, not backward. This sentiment has always been engrained in our culture— from the colonists seizing native land, to the politicians of every political stripe: "Go west, young man!" And by "Go west," they really meant "Look ahead—don't worry about all that stuff you're leaving behind."

Here's what I knew about my father and his side of the family: At Christmastime, they enjoyed drinking a sludgy and highly alcoholic concoction known as a Tom and Jerry. There were nuns who'd rapped his knuckles in middle school. In his hometown, every family had lots of siblings, cousins, aunts, and uncles—quite different from my only-child household. These were my main cultural reference points for "Irish Catholic." They were stories casually told in passing, reminders of my father's storybook beginning before he came to the East Coast.

Elsewhere in our house, Asia was present but not entirely accounted for. When my mother went to bed each night, she knelt in prayer toward a small gold statue of the Buddha as she recited her prayers, softly and quickly. She'd touch my knee as we drove past cemeteries, and whenever I mentioned death, she would mutter in Burmese under her breath. She made me spit on my fingernails every time I trimmed them. Practically speaking, this is what it meant to be half-Burmese: a series of traditions and almost magical-seeming practices I didn't really understand but accepted nonetheless.

Every April is the annual Burmese New Year's water festival of Thingyan. On the streets of Rangoon, men and women and children throw water at one another in celebration of the new year—and to cool off in the middle of the excruciatingly hot dry season. Meanwhile, the immigrant community in and around Silver Spring, Maryland—right outside my home in Washington, D.C.—would traditionally gather in someone's backyard to celebrate. To me, sloshing water around on 54-degree early spring weekends was practically torture. Neighborhood boys, usually aged ten to twelve, had a field day—but they were more excited to taunt me than to celebrate the new year. Armed with plastic buckets brimming with cold water from the garden hose, the boys would unceremoniously hurl water at me. I hated it, and would have much preferred to celebrate the New Year—everybody *else's* new year in December—with the Times Square ball and a glittery, feathered tiara. Each April, as I beelined back to the circle of adults giggling and clucking at my soaked clothing, I felt annoyed and angry that I had to suffer through these stupid humiliations.

I thought of myself as generically American, both in cultural preference (Chips Ahoy!, cartoons) and appearance (T-shirts and sneakers), but occasionally, I was reminded that how I saw myself wasn't necessarily how everyone else saw me. As on the day when I sat at the counter of the American City Diner and the white line cook turned to ask me, while my father was in the bathroom, if I was adopted. I brushed it off, as if this were something I was asked all the time. It most certainly wasn't. Instead of showing my surprise, I laughed to relieve him of how embarrassed he must have been to ask such an awkward question, and responded, "Oh no, my mother's just Asian!"

But he wasn't embarrassed for having asked me that at all. Moments like this were reminders that, to some people, I was *not* generically American.

I had invested fully in the story my parents told me. I considered most everyone—no matter their race, culture, or religion—American, just like me, never minding that we didn't look alike or come from the same places. We were here! And yet the feeling was not always mutual: In the eyes of certain folks, who were universally certain *white* folks, I was not American; I was something else. If my "we" included them, theirs did not include me.

Even then, as a twelve-year-old in the diner drinking a vanilla shake, I recognized the power of this exclusiveness. I deferred to it, respectful. I offered a grinning explanation as to why I didn't look the way some line cook thought the daughter of an average white American should look. In fact, my reply verged on being an apology. The cook's certainty about what was generically

American and what was not generically American seemed to be deeply entwined with something—blood or DNA or place—that was far more definitive than the casual connections I'd forged in my life thus far. I envied his sense of ownership over who was (or must be) a Typical American—his belief regarding who *belonged*—even if it made me feel fairly terrible to have an identity I'd casually assumed and embodied suddenly . . . denied.

How could *I* feel like I belonged? How could I define my identity? Perhaps, I eventually realized, the answer was not in trying to fit myself into the world of generically white Americana, where I would never be at home. But nor was it in joining the suburban Burmese exile community in Silver Spring, which seemed just as distant and had a significant language barrier to boot.

After all, neither my maternal nor paternal backgrounds had held much sway over my sense of self. Luxembourg and Burma were about as familiar to me as Narnia and the North Pole. But when I considered my heritage as a single thing, rather than an either-or proposition in which I had to choose between Rangoon and Esch, these two poles—Burmese and Irish-Luxembourgian—taken *together* offered something entirely, definitively new. And this category of Mixed Race Heritage, this was a place I could belong!

I wouldn't be bound by outdated ideas about identity, some hokey old-timer's notion of what "regular" America looked like. That was the past! My own, new tribe would be as rigorously inclusive as that line cook was exclusive.

My thinking about this brave new identity crystalized on November 18, 1993, when the cover of *Time* magazine heralded "The New Face of America," which kind of (if you squinted) looked like me.[1]

"Take a good look at this woman," the headline dared the reader. "She was created by a computer from a mix of several races. What you see is a remarkable preview of . . . THE NEW FACE OF AMERICA."

Inside was a story that promised to explain "how immigrants are shaping the world's first multicultural society."

I was a sophomore in high school and the cover was a revelation: *I* was the new face of America? Somehow I was an early example, sent from the future to show the people of America what they would all look like a few generations down the road. Just as *Time* promised, these parents of mine—one immigrant plus the child of some immigrants—had unknowingly created the *futureface*. I felt comforted by the idea that, according to this article, I belonged in the world the future promised us: one of cultural and racial inclusion.

When I was in high school, I found a box filled with my mother's old clothes from the seventies. There was a tiny bright green T-shirt emblazoned with orange iron-on letters that spelled out RANGOON RAMONA. It was something my father had made for my mother, based on a nickname that had been retired several anniversaries ago, but here was the perfect shirt for me, futureface. "Rangoon" was the capital of Burma, far away on the other side of the world. "Ramona" was the Old World. The old European world, that is. It dawned on me that I felt lucky. To be Burmese without the Irish-German half was to be *Asian*. To be a descendant of Irish Germans was to be white. Oh, but to be both! To be both was to be the space between them, the whole world that their stories traversed. It was to be the future.

And so here I was, in my mother's RANGOON RAMONA T-shirt, defending not one particular culture but swimming around in the new thing created from the mixture of two. It seemed almost greedy.

On a trip to Hawaii right before college, a local called me a "hapa." What exactly was a hapa? I asked. "It means you're mixed!" he said to me, and the revelation was like having lived your whole life thinking you were a pigeon only to find out you were a toucan. Tropical, ambiguous, interesting. Hapa.

Shortly after college, on a visit to New York, a man in a coffee shop came up and asked me, "What's your blood?" I responded, "O negative," because he deserved a ridiculous answer for an absurd question. The idea that I could name my "blood" was a small-minded concept. Instead, I had started celebrating multiculturalism—just as America had.

Since America's inception by European colonists, the country's culture had been strictly white and male-oriented. Recent leaps toward diversity have been a refreshing, much-needed change from the patriarchy. The shift began with the 1960s cultural studies programs born of protest, starting with the establishment of African American studies. Even white Judeo-Christian scholars started to question whether mainstream culture best represented our dynamic and increasingly diverse society: Didn't women and brown folks play pivotal roles in the building of our democracy, our economy, our history? If there was a common American story, how could it be told without them with any accuracy whatsoever?

By the 1970s, scholars and activists and authors were questioning this incomplete, uniformly white history. In 1980, historian and activist Howard Zinn released his alternative chronicle of our national development, called *A People's History of the United States.* This history acknowledged the labor of slaves, the work of women, the struggles of the native people. The book was about the developments and contributions that happened at the grassroots level, that were sidelined and marginalized— but were no less pivotal. Zinn's text could be taught in classrooms as an alternative to the dusty, one-sided histories of yore, and American liberals were now taking their turn at reframing a story that had been told since the beginning of time.

In my own high school during the early nineties, a steady diet of dead white men—Chaucer, Hawthorne, Donne—began to change. Now we would read literature that included Chinua Achebe's *Things Fall Apart* and Alex Haley's *Roots.* Now we would study Ghana, Mali, the Songhai Empire, and Benin. We would know Africa, because Africa, not just Europe, had birthed America. Knowing this not only made us wiser, it made us stronger: truer to our values, our people, our histories. America was not simply the Stars and Stripes; it was a mosaic, a quilt, a rainbow. There was power in being mixed.

Or at least, that was the idea. Because as soon as my class started reading Langston Hughes's "I, Too," the backlash from white students began.

14

And it wasn't just in my classroom. Conservatives started to attack this new open-minded American canon as a threat to national identity. They blamed immigrants for America's troubles, drawing a firm line in the sand— that imagined line between "Us" and "Them."

But conservatives weren't the only ones to criticize multiculturalism. Liberals recognized that the "melting pot" idea had its own problems: it eliminated the differences between cultures, breaking them down into one mushy stew—and wasn't this, too, a sort of surrender? I remember vaguely toward the end of my high school career being cautioned not to refer to America as a "melting pot" but instead as a "salad bowl"—the idea being that the ingredients in a salad bowl kept their integrity, even though they were mixed. A tomato was still a tomato— even if it was surrounded by lettuce.

Things got even more complicated by the time I went to Brown University—which was, incidentally, the *only* school my parents requested I not apply to. "Political correctness has run amok over there!" my mother declared one autumn Sunday after reading a less-than-flattering story about the school in the *New York Times*. My father didn't really know what precisely constituted political correctness, but sided with her anyway. Naturally, I decided to apply early and chose to attend as soon as the mailman had delivered my acceptance letter. (I had never even seen the campus.)

At my future alma mater, I attempted to navigate the choppy waters of multiculturalism. Would I join the South Asian Students Association? Or did the very existence of this group reinforce the marginalization that it tried to combat? (Answer: I joined but never attended any of the meetings.) I took post-colonial literature classes, and I read the Palestinian intellectual Edward Said's book *Orientalism*.

The generic mantle of "mixed" felt empowering, but curiously . . . weightless. Perhaps because being mixed race wasn't something that was discussed as being an identity, the way singular racial categories frequently were. I knew there was no such thing as a racial history without baggage, but I had no conception of how to reconcile my family's pasts with my present and all the privileges I had that they did not. So I didn't. Somehow, I reasoned that because I was a new thing, a Burmese-Luxembourgian, my role in the American story was unwritten. Ultimately, I chose not to think about the backstories of the European and Asian cultures in my blood. I opted for that most American of paths: forward, to the future, with complete disregard for what had been left behind.

Even as I spread my wings, I always felt like the kid who still played solitaire, if metaphorically. As I grew older, I became better at making friends and finding companions, but these relationships were always partially instrumental: I was trying to stave off loneliness.

"We are born alone, and we will die alone," my father used to recite, in case I had any ideas that my best friends and favorite pets would be joining me in the afterlife. It wasn't what an only child needed to hear over a Saturday-morning bowl of cereal, but this is what he thought of as wisdom, a thing to remember in good times and bad, so he repeated it often and I came to believe it. When my parents finally divorced, some twenty years after they got married, this expression took on even more meaning: my parents' unlikely partnership had ended, and I was truly alone, like an astronaut on a distant planet.

Friendships created connection and rituals, but those friendships, as delightful and nurturing as they were, were born because circumstance threw us together. My friends were my friends for the same reasons two strangers got married and became my parents: we bonded over shared schools or interests or tastes in music, not because we were tied together by blood and tradition. And just like my parents, as conveniently as we had come together, we could be broken apart.

This sense of unrootedness, of fleetingness, followed

me into adulthood. I wondered: How did other people adapt so easily?

The problem I was trying to solve was a personal one, deep inside myself. It was something others, even close friends, couldn't truly solve for me. I didn't have a people. I didn't know where I could find home.

This is something that we are also grappling with as a country: Who are our people? What makes them so? Across the country, people are craving that same sense of belonging I longed for, so many years ago, sitting on the living room floor, playing solitaire—the feeling of self-recognition and camaraderie. I have long recognized the absence of belonging, a questioning loneliness, in myself. And it's split the country around me. We've divided ourselves, segregated our communities into Us and Them in an attempt to feel whole, to better establish who *we* are.

Could I ever find that grounding thing for myself?

After so much time, so many years, spent looking to answer this question, I wondered if what I was looking for was in me already. Instead of trying to be the example of the accepting, mixed-race world I dreamed of for the future, I could go back in time to search my own blood to find my people.

I began contemplating this and how I'd go about it.

I'd never dug into the family archives. I was going to have to learn the stories that unfolded long ago that, in turn, determined my own story. Going on this journey was a chance, at long last, to know myself and where I truly— for real this time—belonged.

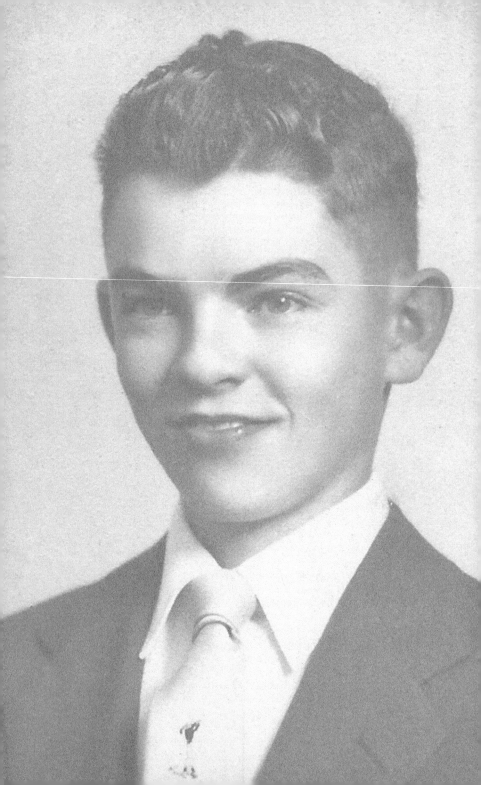

CHAPTER TWO

We talk about our identities—our race, our nation, our neighborhood, our group of like-minded souls—as if they are permanently tied to who we are, a trait formed at birth. I've always known that's not really true. Identity is also something we learn, something we choose, something we have to grow—or lose—along the way. Someone's identity might be a personal decision; it might be imprinted by parents; it might be casually, cruelly assigned in junior high.

Or it might be something that's been tucked away, a mystery that demands exploration, just waiting to be discovered.

For a while, not feeling part of any particular identity group freed me of race and tribe, the powerful and destructive ideas that helped cause so much of the world's misery. Let the other kids roam in cliques across the schoolyard—Alexandra Swe Wagner could glide through life without a herd. Or at least, I thought I could. Because when I was presented with the mystery of heritage and identity, it turned out to be too tempting not to look around. Sure, maybe I'd come across scandals, secrets, family fallouts—but I was going to open that Pandora's box and peer inside anyway, embracing all the wild stuff that flew out of it.

On the day of my First Holy Communion, I got a nose-bleed. I already felt like I didn't belong at the church. I'd barely attended the required religious education classes. I didn't really know any of the Bible passages or the lyrics to the happy Catholic songs that all the other kids in my communion class seemed to know by heart. But there, as I sat in one of the front pews of Holy Trinity Church, wearing the required white dress, my nose started running bright red. Only my father was with me (my mother, who is Buddhist, did not attend the ceremony), which made it even worse: the white frills, the blood, the absurdity of this proceeding, my entrance into Catholicism.

It was at my father's request that I was even doing this

at all. The rest of our neighborhood was off celebrating May Day, a holiday for the pagan rites of spring. The contrast between that jolly May celebration outdoors, and the stiff, very godly Catholic ritual could not have been more obvious. Here I was in a marble hall, eating the body and blood of Christ for the first time, mopping up nose blood with a roll of toilet paper from the church bathroom. I would so much rather have been on Brandywine Street, running down the block in a flower crown and dancing around with kids my age. Why wasn't I out there, twirling around the maypole? Frolicking in the neighbors' front yard seemed more worthwhile than trying to remember Catholic prayers indoors.

I was angry with my father for making me take part in this event. I know he meant to connect me to his family traditions, but it was all happening without much explanation. I hadn't been taught anything about Catholicism, or why communion and church were important in the grand scheme of things. So being shoved into a church all of a sudden felt like reading the middle chapter of a very long history book without knowing what came before and what might follow. I hadn't gone to religion classes— okay, fine, I had been conned into attendance once or twice with the lure of free doughnuts in the church basement, but I had no real connection to whatever was supposed to be taking place at the altar. If this was my heritage, it felt incomplete.

My father had made his own mix-and-match choices about Catholic tradition and social justice, passing down to me Catholic values but not always putting Catholic customs into practice. Being from Iowa, knowing the value of a dollar and the importance of a good handshake—these were all central to my father's identity. Catholic values, as defined by the progressive, anti-poverty wing of the church (rather than the Vatican), were the foundation for my father's political beliefs. He'd wanted to solve the problem of hunger in America and to bring resources to the poor. My dad's sermons about forgiveness, empathy, and charity were convincing. They always stuck with me.

But while my father shaped his life with his religion's most progressive political values, the pomp and circumstance of Catholic ritual were not as important. His political work obsessed him, but the rituals and community of small-town Iowa grew further and further away. And when I came along, he didn't indoctrinate his only child to the ways of the institutional church. He figured a Catholic political education, taught in a series of kitchen table homilies—rather than scheduled religion classes—might suffice.

This was no small loss in the transmission of the Wagner family legacy. The church *was* the legacy, in large part—but it was a legacy mostly denied to me. The institution of the church was the basis of nearly all of my father's own childhood memories: Religion was the bark wrapped 'round his family tree. My father, Carl Robert Wagner, Jr., attended Catholic schools with all of his sisters and brother, and went to a small Catholic college after that. The nuns and priests were his surrogate parents, his disciplinarians, his spiritual guides. His father, Carl Wagner, Sr., made sure his clan prayed each night and attended Mass every Sunday. It was by sharing these rituals that they also found their people.

According to my dad, the tiny town of Lansing, Iowa, had five churches, which were organized mostly around ethnicity. The biggest was the Church of the Immaculate Conception, where everyone was reportedly of Luxembourger, German, or Irish Catholic stock.

"There was an incredible awareness of who was and who wasn't Catholic," he told me. "The Gaunitz brothers"—the owners of the meat market where he worked—"used to constantly make fun of Catholics and call them 'mackerel snappers' because they ate fish on Friday."

Ironically, that mackerel was sold by the one Jewish family in town: Jacob and Rose Erlich, who ran the Lansing fish market. Every Thursday, Jacob and his sister Rose would drive to all the Catholic houses and ring their bells. "Mom would answer the door to see what fish was fresh. Jacob would weigh the fish right there and give them to her," he remembered, with no small amount of nostalgia. "Eating fish on Friday, it was the way things were done in the Catholic church when I was a kid."

Jacob Erlich was the one who urged my father to go to college: "When I was a senior in high school, he must have asked me twenty-five times where I was gonna go to college," my dad recalled. "He encouraged me to do it." I had never heard of Jacob Erlich before; it seemed strange to me that someone who'd played such a pivotal role in my father's life would appear only now, in such a late chapter.

I asked my dad whether the Erlichs might have faced discrimination as the only Jewish family in a one-horse, five-church Christian town. He dismissed the thought entirely: "No, not at all." He was sure. "Jacob and Rose were Jewish . . . but it was irrelevant, really," he proclaimed, as if its lack of relevance to *him* made it definitive.

When my dad was a junior in high school, he competed in the Iowa Oratorical Declamation contest, performing the essay "I Speak for Democracy" by a young woman named Elizabeth Ellen Evans. He won the contest and was asked to reprise the performance in front of a local club for the town businesspeople—among them, Jacob Erlich.

As my dad stood in front of that crowd of clerks and grocers and fishmongers, repeating the essay's simple but heartfelt message about religious tolerance and American identity, Jacob Erlich began to cry. By way of an explanation, my father offered: "I think it was the first time in his lifetime in Lansing—the first time in an honorific way—that Judaism had been referred to." The way I saw it: If Mr. Erlich was moved by this moment of being included, it might be because he'd felt *ex*cluded for so long from this community. But when I asked my father whether this single Jewish family might have somehow been marginalized—or whether their exclusion from the parish had been lonely, or even possibly miserable—his answer was still a firm no.

Instead, my father was insistent that the Erlichs were simply interesting secondary characters in the larger picture of the happy town of Lansing, people who didn't know compromise or hardship. If anything, said Dad, Jacob Erlich's tears illustrated the magnificence of our country, where difference was frequently accepted and could even be a source of pride. This interpretation was less about Jacob Erlich than it was about my father and his town and their generosity. It showed the way the majority wielded their power without—at least to my dad's eye—prejudice. They were white and Christian; they were American, so powerful as to appear invisible, at least to themselves.

And then, out of the blue, that entire narrative was thrown upside down.

"Your aunt Susan thinks we were Jewish," my father mentioned one day in passing, as if everyone had someone in their family who *secretly believed they were Jewish,* "because we had Mogen David wine at Thanksgiving."

That day, my dad's friend Larry Kirk was over at the house, and it was Larry who clarified: "It's a kosher wine."

"I didn't know that," my dad said. "Wine was— No one knew anything about it. Beer was the drink of choice in the Midwest."

Mogen David wine, like its cousin Manischewitz, is a syrupy drink consumed mostly at Passover seder. At the turn of the nineteenth century, Jewish immigrants from the Old World soaked raisins in water and then boiled down the liquid to make their version of wine for Passover dinner. It sounds undrinkably sweet, but it was surprisingly popular.

My father swiftly explained away the kosher wine at

the dinner table of his semi-rural Iowa childhood home. He said drinking an "exotic" wine was probably just his family's attempt at being high class. I furrowed my brow and considered this. It seemed fishy to me: There was no other evidence that he could point to that revealed an interest in upscale, metropolitan custom or experimental dinner-table eating and drinking. In his house, there was fish on Fridays, doughnuts on Sunday, and corn in between.

"My dad was almost a socialist," my father had once explained. "He wouldn't let me join the Boy Scouts—he called it a 'paramilitary organization.' He'd turn on the radio every night at six to listen to the news, and he would always say something to the extent of 'General Motors, General Electric, General Eisenhower!' He was skeptical of power."

With this information about my grandfather in mind, my father's casual explanation about the Jewish wine didn't make sense, not to me. My father's family story had been so incredibly white-bread that the very suggestion of mystery, of lost roots, of secret Jewish ancestry, challenged our conception of the Wagner clan's "traditional" Irish Catholic roots.

My family's bragging rights had till now centered on my far-flung Burmese ancestors on my mother's side— what was more exotic than Burma?—but here was a whole new chapter of possibility. About me. Yes—I was feeling self-involved about it. My first thought upon hearing what I will refer to as the Jewish Theory was to imagine how much more interesting "Burmese Jewish" sounded than "Burmese American." Sure, Judaism was passed down through the maternal line, so, technically speaking, I wouldn't be on-the-official-books Jewish. But, at least in my book, that didn't negate my possibly Jewish lineage. And, hey, if someone was offering a ticket, I was taking it.

But really, what excited me most about this development was the sense of belonging that being Jewish might give me.

I understood "Our Jewish Heritage" to mean something powerful—far more powerful than "Our Iowan Irish Heritage." Maybe, I thought, being Jewish would once and for all answer the question of identity and community. The notion of identity that had been forbidden to me—the idea that I could belong somewhere and find myself in that belonging—suddenly became, I realized with some surprise, a thing that I dearly wanted.

I discussed the Jewish Theory with my second cousin Karl, a college student in New York City. Karl didn't seem tied to any particular part of our family story, and that made him reliable. He also didn't seem to find it odd that I was exhibiting newfound interest in our family tree.

Immediately, I wanted to know what Karl knew about the man who first brought the Wagner family to America: our great-grandfather Henry Wagner. What kind of man was Henry? What kind of woman was his wife, our great-grandmother Anna? Was anything hidden in the treasure trove of family anecdotes that might suggest a lost religion, membership to a forgotten society?

I felt like a detective, desperate not to give away any of my leads. I was greedy for details, biographical sketches, whatever Karl could produce. At some point in the interrogation, in the middle of all the familiar stories of aunts and uncles and Iowa, Karl let slip another tantalizing clue.

Apparently, Great-Grandfather Henry was a fisherman, happy to drop his lines on the banks of the Mississippi River. Some years into his life, on one of his countless trips out on the water, Henry got himself into some kind of trouble. There was an unspecified accident, Karl recounted, and suddenly Henry was heard screaming for help. In Yiddish. As in the High German language of the Ashkenazi Jews.

This knowledge of Yiddish—a language I now discovered was spoken "informally" by my great-grandfather—was obviously unknown to me. My father certainly never made mention of it. But for me, this was all the evidence

I needed. We were Jewish. Or at least, it was *a pretty good bet* that we were Jewish. My father, to my great annoyance, clung to the idea that this was instead some sort of kooky ethnic coincidence, simply evidence of Henry's skill at foreign languages.

And so: I decided to contact my aunt Susan, my father's sister. As the youngest of the six Wagner children, Susan had spent a lot of time alone after her siblings left home. Like me, she grew up as a silent presence, surrounded by adults who didn't always take notice of her. This gave her lots of opportunities to overhear things.

While she had only the dimmest recollections of my great-grandfather Henry and his wife, Anna, she had spent time with my great-uncles and -aunts in a way that the other children hadn't. I asked her what she might recall about any possible Jewish clues, and she emailed me a few weeks later:

> When I was in high school I often visited my uncle
> Leo. He was the youngest and last living of [Henry
> Wagner's] children. Our conversations centered
> on news of my siblings, what I was learning in
> school, and politics, and were accompanied with
> doughnuts and a small jelly glass of Mogen David

wine. Uncle Leo, like Dad, was deeply religious,
but did not hold the parish priests in high esteem.
During one of our less-than-positive conversations
about the local clergy, Leo said, "Well, I'm just an
old Jew." Unfortunately, the conversation went no
further, and I didn't press for details.

It was staggering that Susan could remember—
explicitly!—an admission by someone in the family that
we were Jewish. Here was proof that there was Judaism
in our veins. Unbelievably, no one had followed up! I
didn't understand how you could hear something like this
and remain unfazed. Here was a family that said Christian
prayers every evening after dinner. A family that went
to Mass each Sunday without fail. A clan of children for
whom Catholic school was the only existence they'd ever
known in a town with a single Jewish family—a group of
semi-strangers—and yet a revelation regarding their own
Judaic roots was met without blinking, as if it had been an
observation about the weather.

Could there be a more sinister reason that my father
had resisted following up about his allegedly Jewish heritage? He might have gone on at length to me about the
Erlich family and what wonderful people they were . . .
but they were clearly outsiders. And perhaps my father's

fond recollections about how "well" the lone Jewish family was integrated into Christian Lansing society masked the fact that everyone in town, including my father, was aware that they *were* treated as different. I wondered if the suggestion that he was different, too, didn't strike him as an exciting revelation but rather as a threat. It would challenge what my father comfortably thought of as his white, Catholic heritage.

What did it mean for the Wagners not to be Catholic? It was hard to imagine, given the importance of the church in my father's home life and his cultural orientation. It was therefore cause for quiet fear. And the most efficient way to deal with the fear was to do everything in your power to avoid it. So my father brushed the theory aside, willed it away.

But I was ready to get at the truth. Not simply because I had a natural inclination toward detective work in general, but because it had awakened something in me. I was newly woke to the possibility that after all this time adrift I might now connect to something deeper and solve those longstanding questions: Where did I belong and who did I belong to?

To be Jewish was to possess an identity rooted in the earliest stories recorded by the human hand! To be part of its traditions and practices and part of a heritage that had always seemed so deep-rooted thrilled me. It seemed like a gift—especially compared with my hazy line of lineage. How could I not care about this? I was consumed by a need to know.

This need to know is what fuels other people, too, in the global search for identity. Perhaps that explains the explosion in genealogy services and genetic testing to determine ancestry, which is now a billion-dollar industry.[1] Maybe, in a world that at times can feel quite lonely, everybody has a basic desire to find themselves. We feel we are *all* entitled to an Ancestor Quest of our very own. I, for one, felt that not only did I need to know the answers, I also *deserved* to know them.

As I plotted the next stages of my investigation, I started to wonder: Why did I care so much about my paternal relatives' history? What about my Burmese roots? On my father's side, the mystery was intriguing and called for an epic wandering into the past, where I could question the dead (or at least look for clues about their lives). But on my mother's side, it was my own fault that I was in the dark. Everyone who could tell me what I wanted to know was still living; they just needed to be asked.

My family represented two approaches to the puzzle of identity and belonging. Both sides told American tales, concerned with the future, not the past. But there were clear differences, too. My father's history was the story of American assimilation, made all the more straightforward for his emigrating from a Western country. His family had crossed the Atlantic and landed right in the heart of America, white and Christian. But in trading some specific European story for a broader American version—who knows what was lost?

My mother's story was also an immigrant tale, but it was not so clearly one of assimilation. She didn't look like the so-called average American, and her traditions, language, and mannerisms that placed her as a person who had left someplace else to come here. She and her mother had fled Burma when it met its ruin, but they remained loyal to their memory of their native country. If you asked my mother what was really wrong with life in Burma, she was hesitant to speak out against it. There was no poisonous tone in her wistful recollections, except when she spoke of the emergencies that had pushed our family out at the very end.

As I started reflecting on my Burmese heritage in my new Ancestor Quest, it occurred to me that in my mother there was a Burmeseness rooted in blood and land that might equally be thought of as an identity, a tribe, like the one I sought.

I had been intrigued by the Jewish Theory. It suggested, most significantly, that in the Wagner family's

American assimilation, something might have been lost. And I wanted badly to recover it.

In other words, the formerly relaxed futureface hapa was suddenly fixated firmly on identity and genealogy. I wanted definitive proof that I was not alone, that I belonged. But where and with whom? It was a mystery to be solved—several mysteries, to be honest—and I loved mysteries. I was on the case: telephone, magnifying glass, library card, passport in hand.

CHAPTER THREE

I began this adventure where most everyone begins any adventure: at home. My parents divorced long ago, and though they had finally reached a point where they could once again share holiday dinners or gossip on the phone about me, their only child, I decided to approach them separately to keep things simple.

My father's side of the family had been large. His parents and two of his siblings had passed away, though, and all the surviving relatives were (relatively) young. That meant that getting to the root of who we were was going to require work beyond Facebook messages. Complicating this was the fact that my father wasn't all that close with his family anymore. Here I was, looking to better know the ghosts of past Wagners, while my father and

I were somewhat out of touch with our living relatives. How had we let things get to this point? I had no siblings. Calling aunts and uncles and cousins with whom I hadn't spoken in years to ask what they remembered about our family made me shy. Reconnecting to family was the purpose of this entire project, but when faced with the prospect of interviewing my father's family, I felt queasy.

So I began with my mother's family on the Burmese side. My grandmother had mostly raised me, and we were in regular communication. The branches on this side of the family tree were still very much tangled up together. Perhaps this was because, as recent immigrants, my mom's relatives had felt bonded to one another, with family as protection in their strange new home. Perhaps this was because of Asian tradition, which dictated that we take care of our elders. (For example, my mother's mother lived with us for several years at a certain point, while my father's mother moved into a retirement home when she aged.) Or perhaps it was just because of geography: my mother's immediate family moved to America and settled on the East Coast, and we saw one another frequently.

I went first to the oldest person in our family, the one whose memory could stretch the farthest back in time: my grandmother. She was not like other grandmothers. Most grandmothers did not play poker through the night. Nor did they hide stinking durian fruits in their kitchens. Most grandmothers did not covet diamonds and forget birthdays. Most grandmothers did not try to get arrested while protesting in front of the Burmese embassy.

Before the internet and Twitter, before hashtags and streaming video, she was the member of our family most fully briefed on all the developments in Burma. When the military junta shot and killed thousands of peaceful protesters following a massive protest on August 8, 1988—a significant turning point in contemporary Burmese politics—the person to phone our house with the news was my grandmother. "There's been a coup!" she declared. (I wasn't entirely sure what a coup was then, but it sounded dramatic. I soon found out that it meant a takeover, an uprising of Burmese civilians against the brutal Burmese government.) It was she who, even well into her eighties, met with and supported Burmese pro-democracy activists who had been exiled after the coup.

When a group of aged Burmese men—uncles, as they were known—formed an exile government known as the National Coalition Government of the Union of Burma, my grandmother was their treasurer. She was an honorable matriarch of the new pro-democracy movement—a position she'd adopted from her perch in America.

I imagine that she was able to combine this Burmese activism with her status as a United States citizen because while my grandmother considered herself a fully integrated member of American society—buying sweaters at department stores, staying informed on members of Congress—she didn't really consider herself "an American." She would often begin sentences with "We Burmese . . ." to make clear the line between where she lived and who she actually was.

Since embarking on my Ancestor Quest, I viewed this connection to Burma in a new way. My grandmother, like my father and his nostalgic stories of Iowa, had that thing I wanted so much: a single, clear identity, one that strengthened her beliefs and stirred her to action. Her certainty in her beliefs, her effortless navigation between worlds . . . I wanted to find that same committed sense of myself.

For nearly all of her ninety-eight years, my grandmother had been keenly, fully *alive*. She could be selfish and bossy (she felt no embarrassment in being waited on by my mother). She could also be kind. In our relationship, her generosity mostly took the form of food (breakfasts of Burmese yellow peas and rice) and jewelry (gold bangles). But she made it clear that if she hadn't approved of who I had grown up to be, I would not have gotten her emerald rings.

While she was undeniably picky, she didn't worry about unpleasant things—instead, each day, she rolled her Buddhist prayer beads through her gnarled, tiny hands, drank what we roughly estimate to be four glasses of wine, and slept soundly for eleven hours a night. She watched the news religiously, and she couldn't stand Republicans.

And she was an excellent source of information. While other people in their nineties had a hard time recognizing faces in front of them, she could still answer questions about events that had taken place decades ago. She could recollect the faintest details: the name of a principal who had shown her father kindness *at the turn of the twentieth century,* or the piping hot chicken noodle soup she tasted on her very first trip to America *in 1951.* Born in 1917, she had seen most of the twentieth century, and it was impossible to summarize her particular type of twentieth-century life, one that had survived colonial rule and dictatorial regimes to emerge, finally, into the beginnings of a democracy.

My grandmother's name was Mya Mya Gyi, and she was born in Pakokku in 1917. In that year, Europe was invading countries around the world and imposing its power on them. The continent was also being shattered by a devastating world war. For comparison, this was the time my grandfather on my father's side was shipping off to Europe to fight in World War I as part of the 163rd Depot Brigade, leaving from Camp Dodge in Johnston, Iowa.

My grandmother Mya Mya, meanwhile, was born

under the British flag. Burma—along with India, Pakistan, and Bangladesh—was part of the British Raj (meaning, under the rule of the British crown) referred to in those days as India. And yet to suggest to my grandmother that her family was Indians—or Brits—would seem laughably absurd. "We were Burmese, of course!" she'd protest. But the soil beneath their feet was not their own, the way it once had been. Their land had been snatched up, and suddenly belonged to someone else.

Containing more than 135 ethnic groups within its borders, Burma was a diverse and cosmopolitan culture from the beginning, and that wasn't even counting the Jewish Baghdadis who set up Rangoon's shops or the Italian traders who came to King Mindon's court in the mid-1800s. There were the Chin, Kachin, Shan, and Karen people—each with their own dress and cuisine, and often their own armies.

If there was one thing that united Burma's many different tribes, it was the hatred they shared for the ruling military junta. The junta had taken power in the early 1960s and engaged in a brutal campaign of oppression against the country's ethnic minorities—a battle so bloody and violent that it would keep Burma at war with itself for nearly half a century. But beyond this enemy, it would be difficult to find a common cause among the various ethnic groups.

Class was the main difference between my Burmese family and families from other tribes. Of all these ethnic groups, my grandmother was Bamah, and there's a reason the country was (kind of) named after her people: They were wealthy, perched at the top of the social and financial ladder. My grandmother was the daughter of a Burmese civil servant named U Myint Kaung—a man who bought three pairs of leather shoes with his first sizable paycheck, and introduced the family to Christmas stockings and whiskey cake from Rowe & Co., the luxury department store in downtown Rangoon.

When my grandmother informed me of her family's wealth and taste for Western goods, it cleared up a lot. Now I understood a bit more why she directed her anger toward the Indians, not the British . . . even though the British were the ones who had invaded her homeland. She gave the British a pass for their behavior because they were the ones who imported luxury items (that her family could afford) to Burma and showed her a glittering world beyond the Burmese shores. The Indians, on the other hand, were geographical neighbors who existed separately from the Burmese, and were decidedly *different*—at least as she saw them.

My great-grandfather U Myint Kaung had European tastes, but he wore those English shoes with traditional Burmese dress, like an *aingyi* and *gaung baung.* He was raised in the Wesleyan Methodist mission schools and spoke fluent English but remained a devout Buddhist, one who had no issue giving up his worldly possessions near the end of life to become a monk (much to his wife's chagrin). Nevertheless, he spoiled my grandmother awfully.

She was the youngest of the family, the last daughter in a house of six children. Daw Tin Pu and Daw Tin U were the eldest daughters, and when it came time for a third child, their mother very badly wanted a son. She was instead gifted another daughter, whom she unapologetically named Kyi Thein, which means (roughly) "No more"—as in "Please: No more girls." Soon enough, another daughter, Kyi Kyi Nyein, was born. Apparently, her name was an even firmer plea to whoever might be listening: According to my grandmother, her name is best translated as "Seriously, stop—no more after this."

Finally, a son was born. He was named Aung Myo—a more generous name than his older sisters received. *Aung* means "successful," and Myo was for the town in which he was born: Maymyo, a picturesque little hill town in northern Shan State.

Relieved to have a boy, my grandparents didn't mind so much when their next daughter was born: my grandmother. They named her Mya, for the emerald, a stone of "calm contentment." She was lucky not just in her name, but in everything else, too.

"I was introduced at a young age to Cadbury chocolate," she recounted in the way that other children had been introduced to arithmetic or *Aesop's Fables*. "And we had bananas at teatime," she boasted, suggesting these tropical fruits were a luxury, even a sign of superiority. At the age of sixteen, my grandmother begged her father for a car, a relatively new machine that had only recently come into existence, in 1931. "I was quite spoiled!" she admitted.

If doling out chocolate and bananas and Dodge motorcars at a young age did anything, it gave Mya Mya a sense of entitlement and high-class taste. She saw this as a way to distinguish herself from everyone else. It did, in some ways, prepare her for the future. When she fled Burma nearly forty years later with nothing and had to start over, knowing the taste of milk chocolate and the thrum of an American motor was like currency, a way of easing into the West.

And even for me, these objects and acquisitions were reassuring proof that we were somebody. My grandmother's charmed life in Burma—as she described it to me—was a blessed existence that had followed my family from the life they left behind on the humid deltas of Rangoon . . . all the way to the Atlantic coast of the United States.

Mya Mya's mother, my great-grandmother, Daw Thet Kywe, was adventurous and ambitious, captivated by metropolitan life. She requested that the British transfer her husband, a man from dusty Pakokku in Upper Burma, to the leafy delta city of Rangoon, where she traveled several times a year on shopping trips to buy diamonds. Their first city residence in the capital was a luxury two-bedroom apartment on Fifty-Second Street, one with running water and what was known then as an English toilet.

My grandmother's three eldest sisters were educated in English missionary schools only until the fourth standard, roughly tenth grade. She and her sister Nyein, on the other hand, went unusually far in their schooling. In Burmese society (as in the United States in the 1920s and '30s), young women did not tend to advance into higher education, let alone graduate school. My grandmother began college at the age of sixteen, when she entered Rangoon University. Nyein graduated second in her class at Rangoon Law School. Despite the strangely misogynistic names my great-grandmother gave my great-aunts, women were treated as full, voting members of the household.

"My sisters smoked—and they liked English food,"

my grandmother told me. "My oldest read the newspaper every day, cover to cover. And she could talk about anything."

My grandmother and her sisters quarreled with one another in the catty, upper-crusty fashion of characters in Victorian novels. Instead of empire-waist dresses, there were *longyis*. In place of tea and scones, it was bananas and biscuits. My mother also recounted impossibly romantic stories about her own adolescence in Burma: games of lawn tennis and croquet, chic embassy parties under twinkling lights, the fragrance of frangipani blossoms wafting through the air as she walked to school. She could still smell the soil after the monsoons, remembering vividly how she would use a giant palm leaf as an umbrella when the rains arrived. Their lives were both charmed and charming—or so they said.

My grandmother Mya Mya eventually left home and settled down. Never one to be plagued by self-doubt, she announced to me that she was "quite popular," and by that she meant "I had a whole lot of boyfriends." Her older sister scolded my grandmother to watch herself. "You should be prim and proper like a Buddhist girl brought up by a decent family. Don't spoil our name. You should behave yourself. Don't flirt with all these people!"

Ultimately, Grandma Mya Mya married a man named U Thant Gyi, a family friend and (scandalously) a widower ten years her senior, patriarch of his own clan of four children. U Thant Gyi, my grandfather, was unfailingly gentle and good-natured. He was a relatively powerful government official in the Burmese education department, happy to indulge his wife's whims. His marriage to my grandmother was a successful one. They had two children together and stayed married until the end.

Here was where our stories—my grandmother's and my own—finally intersected. I knew my grandfather, though only briefly. Before he died, I was nearly three years old and carried around with me a bottle of children's pink Tinkerbell nail polish, which he graciously allowed me to paint on his fine, dark Burmese hands. Even as a child, I remember being struck by the generosity of this gesture (my father would never have allowed the same), and this quiet kindness remains the most significant (and, to be honest, the only) trait I remember about him. That and a fondness for butterscotch candies.

All the tiny details my grandmother could recount about life back then were intoxicating and pleasant, but maybe idealized. I had certain information—but what did I *really* know, except what she chose to share? Was there more that was being hidden?

So I began my own research to fill in the blanks, to

better understand what was happening outside of the plush interior of the family's Dodge motorcar. After all, the things happening elsewhere—which was to say, in the streets outside their happy and luxurious home—were terrible enough to force my family out of Burma . . . forever. Somehow, their sweet lives turned into a voyage of flight and exile.

Perhaps this was why Burma still felt so distant to me—I was romanced by the glossy storytelling, but it had kept me at arm's distance from the country itself, and why my family was no longer there. It was impossible to make a connection to Burma when the stories I heard about it were so one-sided. The world in which I lived seemed wholly at odds with my blissful Burmese heritage. If I really was going to find out whether these were my people, I needed to know exactly what was happening when my family lived there—especially at a time when so much was changing. Burmese independence from the British was right around the corner, and modern Burma's slide into oblivion was about to begin.

What turned a country with a booming economy and an educated population—not to mention a well-regarded independence movement—into a place of nearly unrecognizable hope and despair in just a few short years? What caused a generation of Burmese, including my family, to abandon those sweet-scented frangipani blossoms and those night markets, the bustling shopping centers and fragrant curries from home, for a cold, unknown place on the other side of the world . . . and never look back?

My mother and grandmother never expressed a single sentence of regret about leaving Burma behind, yet they remembered the place with reverence. I couldn't make sense of it and realized I didn't understand the circumstances in Burma when they left. How divided was the population? Who was in power? What did the rest of the world know about what was going on?

No one in my family seemed to have been paying close attention, or their recollections appeared to be full of omissions. I had to know. At this point in my career as a journalist, I understood that old-timey stories were rarely simple, or purely uncomplicated and happy. It always rang alarm bells when anyone got wistful about the good times. In reality, those could actually be pretty bad times for quite a few other people, especially the characters outside the immediate story line.

The stories I'd been told about home, or at least the edits from my father's and mother's sides, had been remarkably free of complications. Could that really have been true?

I already knew the answer to that. Life in the home country couldn't have been entirely rosy; after all, we weren't there anymore—we'd left! I started searching the internet, ordering out-of-print books and obscure volumes of history that could provide a window onto Burma in the great period when my family lived there.

My cousin Geoff had been a Fulbright scholar in Burma and immersed himself in all manner of historical research, and after some begging, he agreed to help me in my search. We were discussing our family history one afternoon when he mentioned that U Myint Kaung, Mya Mya's father and my great-grandfather, had worked as a director of Burma's co-operative societies. I had no idea what these "co-operative societies" were, but I nodded, and he kept talking. (Otherwise, Geoff would have grasped how obviously unprepared I was to start this research.)

"I think the co-ops were kind of a failure?" he offered, as if he also wasn't quite sure what they were.

I couldn't offer my cousin a yes or no, but I remember thinking this was strange: failure was not something that had ever been mentioned when it came to our family's days of triumph and banana snacks. Failure wasn't associated with our family at all. We had been privileged and successful, focused on achievement. I'd found a snag in the carefully woven story of our family. So I pulled it.

PART II

BULLET HOLES
AND ASHES

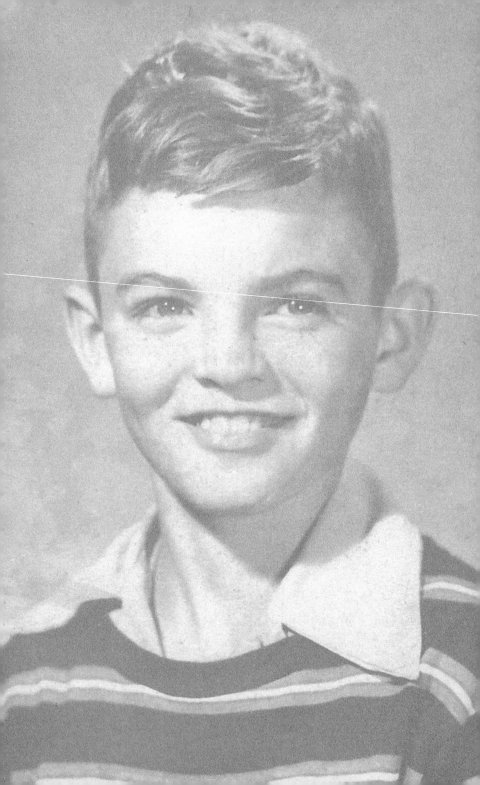

CHAPTER FOUR

As it turns out, I would unravel the story of my maternal great-grandfather's homeland—and discover that it was not some sort of perfect world, but a place that shared my ongoing problem: a crisis of identity. Who are we? Who belongs here? These were familiar questions to me: determining who my own people were was a problem that had plagued me since I was a kid.

My personal quest sent me back to Burma. I'd need to learn about the crisis that had splintered the country, had broken the world apart and spun my family halfway across the globe to the place I was born. But I didn't know all this yet. To understand it, I had to first find my great-grandfather—the person filled with passions and fears and doubts, not just the patriarch of the mystical good ol' days.

I had long imagined Burma's lush, blooming natural world. I could imagine the papery white flowers of the teak trees that began to bloom when the rains arrived in June, until the downpours faded in August. But there was also a dark story behind the natural beauty, one that I had not imagined: for much of the twentieth and early twenty-first century, the ruling military junta had exploited these tall hardwood trees. They sold the teak wood to Europeans, who used it to make outdoor furniture or boat decking for the rich. The military junta used that money from the West to support their dictators in the East.

And then, streaking the rock formations of Burma's jungles,[1] there was the jade—green sodium aluminum silicate believed by the Chinese to be the bridge between heaven and hell. Demand for the semiprecious stone was high, and Burma had plenty to sell. My grandmother and mother had bangles made of the stuff, and I could still hear the way they made soft clinking sounds when rubbed together. Burma's jade still accounts for nearly three-quarters of the global supply, and continues to be extracted in conditions that are brutal and dangerous for workers.

But back in the late nineteenth century, before great-grandfather U Myint Kaung had purchased his first pair of leather dress shoes, and when the British were just beginning their takeover of Burmese tribes (the Bamah, the Kachin, the Shan, the Chin), the export that put his country on the map had its humble origins in the fertile deltas of the Irrawaddy River. Rice—Asia's staple crop and Burma's mainstay—brought this corner of Southeast Asia international acclaim.

In 1869, the opening of the Suez Canal created a passage between the Mediterranean Sea and Red Sea. Ships traveling from the port of Rangoon no longer had to circumnavigate Africa to reach the markets of Europe. Now, the voyage, which had previously taken six months,[2] could be completed in just five weeks. Building the canal cost many, many lives: tens of thousands of Egyptians died slicing open that waterway from the Red Sea to the Mediterranean, a fact that barely seemed to concern the Europeans.

Above all, the Europeans were eager to seize goods from Asia and Africa and bring them back to their countries to sell. European cities were rapidly industrializing and modernizing. From Amsterdam to Paris to Brussels, new technology, machines, and factories were changing the way people worked. Increasingly, people moved into urban areas for financial opportunities. And these growing urban populations needed food. Rice entered

Europe through the port cities of Hamburg and Rotterdam, Gdańsk, and Bremen[3]—not far from landlocked Luxembourg, where Henry Wagner would soon depart for America.

Amid these changes, Burma became an agricultural powerhouse.

In the past, Burmese kings had restricted the export of rice, choosing to keep the grain within the country. Now, the British saw dollar signs and set about conquering the area, which came to be known as the "rice bowl."[4] The battles that followed were knotty and complicated. The first British invasion of Burma began shortly after the Burmese made advances toward British India, conquering the kingdoms of Manipur and Assam in 1821. In response, the Brits declared the kingdoms of Cachar (in Assam) and Jaintia (in northeast India) to be under their protection, setting the stage for confrontation: The First Anglo-Burmese War began in 1824.

The British had already invaded and colonized India, forcing the country's people to assist their further plans for colonialization in Burma. There would be three wars between the Burmese monarchy and the British, culminating on November 27, 1887. The British had overthrown the last Burmese king, and, on this day, triumphantly (for them, at least) lowered the Burmese flag. To the horror of the Burmese people, the British Union Jack flag was soon waving over the teak roofs of the palace compound instead. The Burmese, like my great-grandfather, were now educated in British schools, taught to speak the English language, and otherwise forced to adapt to the colonial powers. The port of Rangoon quickly became a major shipping outpost, bringing in money for the British (and for a few well-connected, high-powered Burmese).

Burma, now a British colony, may have seemed a willing participant in the global trade, but behind the scenes a steep price was being paid by the Burmese themselves. From 1885 until 1910, rice production in Burma went from a few hundred thousand tons to 1.5 million tons.[5] Rice was its own kind of misery. The seeding and sowing, the threshing and harvesting by hand—it was intensely difficult, backbreaking manual labor. Tens of thousands of dark-skinned laborers were forced into a permanent hunch at harvest time. Seeds, fertilizer, and irrigation equipment were expensive. Burmese farmers struggled to cover the costs of growing the crop on their land. The amount of cash they needed to spend to even start producing this much rice was overwhelming.

With no real banking structure to support the money loans, the farmers turned to *chettiars*. Chettiars were moneylenders from southern India who had left for Burma, seeing an open market for their trade.[6] The chettiars would lend money out to farmers, but should the farmer be unable to pay back the loan, the land became property of the chettiar. This put farmers in an uncomfortable position. After all, rice productivity went up and down with the seasons, harvests were unpredictable, and interest rates were high. Property was turned over to the moneylenders, and farmers who had owned land for generations became tenants of greedy landowners who had no interest in knowing what it was like to be a rice farmer. It was a bad deal for the moneylenders; it was a bad deal for the farmers of Burma.

I had never, ever been interested in agricultural economics. Nor did I concern myself with Burmese crop yields or farming policy. But the subject of nineteenth-century Indo-Burmese moneylending was surprisingly interesting! Because it was mine. It was part of my family story. And for the first time, I could see how the titanic events in global history (plus the more regional history of Burma) were all part of my ancestral tale. The opening of the Suez Canal, the colonization of Upper Burma, the appetite for rice in the lowlands of Europe—these massive abstract forces that shaped the world were no longer far away, no longer something that just affected an unseen population in a general sweeping fashion. These tumultuous developments had hit my own family's backyard.

Maybe this was why so many people were so intoxicated by the practice of self-discovery: *Who we are* is a product of battles fought long before us. The winners and losers from centuries ago determine our very existence. Go back far enough, and you'll realize that your ancestors and their lives were inevitably part of a much grander narrative: the history of the world itself.

The more I read, the more I realized that I had a stake in all of it—colonialism, war, the British Empire, the succession of Burmese monarchs, the rain in Rangoon. Within those epic forces was the thread of my family story. At their center was Great-Grandfather U Myint Kaung, a man who made decisions, chose certain paths, and came to be a certain way thanks to the random chaos of history. To seek answers in reference books would not be enough. I had to get down to the personal, to understand what specifically he'd done (or tried to do).

Of course, everyone wants to believe that their ancestors were the winners, the day savers and unsung heroes—or that if they were the losers, they were the blameless, noble ones, the ones fighting to keep the world from falling apart. But who were they really? Were they innocent, or were they predators? Did they do the right thing or the very wrong one? I'd have to ask: What role did my people play in our newly discovered Burmese drama?

Throughout the world, the Great Depression (1929–39) brought on poverty and hunger. In Burma, tensions between the farmers and the lenders reached an all-time high. Chettiars owned more and more of the country's land, 25 percent by 1938. It was putting it mildly to say that this chafed at the national identity of the Burmese.

The British, sensing tension between poor Burmese farmers and wealthier chettiar landlords, installed a system. They decided to find a way to finance rice production without including chettiars, while also schooling the Burmese in the ways of thrift and "Christian responsibility." The British called this the "co-operative credit societies," a three-tiered system designed to produce virtue, credit, and rice.

The co-ops fell into three tiers—here's where it gets tricky.

At the bottom of the ladder were credit societies (made up of individuals and households).

Managing them, at the middle tier, were the credit unions, composed of *several* credit societies, who were supposed to assess whether community members should be allowed to receive loans.

And at the very top of the ladder were the banks (chief among them the provincial bank), which were controlled by the British—and which, when necessary, lent to the middle-tier credit unions.

My great-grandfather worked at the essential point of the whole system: the credit union. U Myint Kaung's job was to make sure money was going to the right people: Burmese with "money sense" who could manage to pay off a loan.

It was a pyramid structure—one that was supposed to be rooted in trust and community responsibility. You could already see where there were problems with this plan: If the credit societies lent to people with no real money sense, or if the credit union didn't audit, or thoroughly research, the financial reliability of the individuals it was lending to, well, then . . . that money couldn't just disappear. Someone was still gonna have to pay for it.

These so-called societies boomed in the early 1920s across Burma. But by 1925, the "cooperative movement was clogged with bad Societies" and loans were being made "too easily."[7] My grandfather, U Myint Kaung, was directly implicated in this failure. By 1932, the all-important provincial bank had been closed down.

In the eyes of the British committee tasked with investigating what went wrong, the Burmese were simply too "polite" to turn down bad candidates for loans—too generous to say no to their neighbors and fellow farmers who were looking for money. U Myint Kaung and the other supervisors at the credit unions had performed faulty audits (or none at all), and apparently compensated for these unfortunate financial decisions by covering them up. These supervisors were declared to be "untrained, uneducated in co-operative banking or co-operative principles and unfit to be let loose amongst any body of co-operators."[8]

Terms such as "untrained" and "let loose" should give you a sense of the disrespect with which the British treated the Burmese supervisors who ran their co-operatives incorrectly. They thought of the Burmese as less than human; animals to be trained. Not that the Burmese had ever asked to be a part of the British colonial banking system to begin with.

So the bottom of the co-operative society pyramid was filled with careless calculations and widespread confusion. A second, more far-reaching report again focused on Burmese incompetence as the fundamental problem: "In Burma, the character of the people is such that a system of official control cannot succeed." It was as if the British had basically given up on an entire country.[9]

In trying to get a wider look at my family history, this is what I discovered: my great-grandfather participated in a dishonest and broken system, one that destroyed the fortunes of many of his fellow countrymen. But if you asked anyone in my family if they thought that U Myint Kaung had been a noble, powerhouse government minister, they'd have said yes without hesitation. My grandmother glossed over a lot of details in her retelling of our family history. She proudly referred to her father's checkered career as an impressive accomplishment.

Did she not know that the co-operative societies were . . . a disaster? Did we not know our people were part of a failing system that ruined the lives of many people who were poor? Or did we just not care? I cared, and it pained me to think of my great-grandfather as someone who'd brought so many Burmese to their knees, courtesy of a failed banking system. (I, unlike the British assessors, was not going to pin the blame on a character flaw in the Burmese people. The system itself was clearly faulty and badly managed.)

More than that, I was shocked that this history had been entirely hidden until now. But I had to admit that learning this somehow also made U Myint Kaung real, in a way that all the other stories about him had not: He had tried and he had failed. Just like I had, just like everybody in the world in which I lived. Shame and catastrophe were hard to face, but they also humanized my ancestors. More so than my grandmother's rose-colored remembrances.

Discovering the mess that was the Co-operative Societies Experiment, and U Myint Kaung's participation in it, definitely explained my great-grandfather's decision to leave behind his worldly possessions and head up to the monastery to devote his life to Buddhist meditation. This was a common practice in Burmese society—the pursuit of an existence devoid of greed. He was done with the material world.

According to my mother, after having relinquished his ties to the family and spent some unspecified amount of time at the monastery, U Myint Kaung got word that his wife had begun the unsavory practice of moneylending— making small loans and then charging interest, the very thing he had worked to end by setting up the farmers' co-operatives in Upper Burma. As it turns out, my great-grandmother had also lost her money in Burma's great financial collapse—U Myint Kaung might have known the banks were about to collapse, but he refused to give his own family special treatment. If the Burmese were suffering, then that would include our family as well.

My grandmother recalled that U Myint Kaung, upon learning that his wife was lending money, came down from the monastery. "He marched down the hill to our home and said to his wife: 'Are you starving? Do you want for anything?' She protested—vaguely—and then begrudgingly admitted she did not want for anything, nor was she starving.

" 'Well, then,' " he said, " " 'don't bargain so much.' "

And he turned and went back up the hill. She never charged interest again.

Maybe he was now convinced that the path to redemption was in selflessness, in commitment to the community. Fine, those British knew a lot about making shoes and whiskey cake, but they didn't understand my great-grandfather's countrymen. And they certainly weren't in any position to make pronouncements about the true nature of the Burmese.

Even if he was not good at his job, U Myint Kaung appeared to have been an intensely moral person. For me, he exists only in stories, and therefore these stories—told mostly by my grandmother—are all I have to understand his motivations. But I think he must have been scarred by what happened to his country's economy and what he had done to help cause its failure. I also believe that through the end of his life, he held on to the ideals that brought him to this line of work in the first place.

As the British and Burmese were striving to improve the economy, Burma became increasingly unstable. Burma is one country in the same way that Iraq is one country, which is to say it's not. It is a collection of contested land that's been fought over for decades. Burma's borders were drawn arbitrarily over time and in the aftermath of battle, by conquerors and colonialists alike. The tensions between different ethnic groups—the Chin and the Shan, the Karen and the Kachin—while already significant, were under remarkable strain in the declining years of colonialism, right as my grandmother came of age.

There was a steep cost to Burma's forever war with itself. Ethnic minorities had been uprooted and forced to the margins. There was conflict and violence between tribes. There were also targeted campaigns of violence launched by the military regime against minorities. People were forced to live in refugee camps that were as big as sprawling cities, without adequate resources, for years on end. These Burmese were not Bamah Burmese—they were Kachin or Chin or Shan or Karen or another tribe.

My people were not in these refugee camps. They were not left in misery and squalor, but had instead escaped it, because of their money and education and luck. Their being able to avoid hardship, and to distance themselves from the less fortunate, was evidence of the power of circumstance. How quickly, and easily, one could go from feeling pride in one's self to feeling superiority over others, from celebration of one's self to dismissal of others. Even as I recognized this, even as I grew older and more aware of how vigilant you need to be to push back the dark impulse to separate Us from Them, there was still something in *me* that clutched at our good fortune, however deep down, as I thought about Burma's miseries. The distinction between the different tribes, each feeling superior to the other, was a refuge—albeit a sinister one.

I was trying to find meaning in connecting my family story to blood and land, but blood was precisely the thing dividing the land, carving it into smaller subgroups and territories. Blood was the thing that would continue to cause division, deepening the cracks of difference in society and tearing apart the Burma that my mother and grandmother could still dream so vividly about. It was the seed of our despair.

My grandmother felt connected to Burma—but not to the whole country, just to her slice of it, her ethnic group, her class. Even after the British colonial powers left the country on January 4, 1948, Burma's inner conflict was escalating. In fact, simmering race tension could be found right in our kitchen.

"We had an Indian cook who made the most delicious curry," my grandmother wistfully recalled. Then she offered—always—this caveat: "And he robbed us blind."

From these aromatic and lusty recollections, I could very nearly taste that curry. In my adolescence, I ate soggy grilled cheese sandwiches and limp tater tots in the school cafeteria; my mother's school lunchtime, on the other hand, was full of piping hot vindaloos and dals, all prepared by the same masterful hand of the family cook. But the story always ended in the same refrain: he robbed the family blind! The talented cook was dismissed, taking with him all those curries and vindaloos—and what a loss this was. Who was that Indian cook? No one ever mentioned his name, only the dishes he prepared.

From the outset of the Indian-Burmese relationship, many Burmans, including my grandmother, referred to Indians as *kalas*. The term is extremely offensive. Its origins may be from the Sanskrit word *kula*—meaning "caste man"—or *kala,* for "black man." Or it may be from the Burmese *ka la*—the term for "coming from overseas." Even after half a century in the United States, my grandmother always referred to Indians as *kalas,* which we American-born descendants didn't quite understand. As it turns out, she might have been calling them, basically, "house negroes," a derogatory (and unacceptable) term for African American workers in decades past.

By the early 2000s, my grandmother had officially lived in America for decades. She had gay friends dating back to the 1970s—friends with whom she drank cocktails after work. She spoke glowingly of the young black men who delivered groceries to her small one-bedroom on Capitol Hill in the 1960s during the Jim Crow era, and as she retold these stories, over time they went from being "young black men" to "young African American men." She fully grasped the importance of the language around identity.

So she knew the power of identification, and the way it contributed to the racial hierarchy in the United States, one where educated whites were allegedly at the top of the pyramid. Among the immigrant classes, Asians were often looked down on as reclusive, tribal, clinging to the ways of the Old World. She was not going to be lumped in with elderly people who grew more conservative and closed-minded with age. She went out of her way to promote her respect for sexual and racial minorities, for people who faced adversity in America because they were not white. This open-mindedness, as much as her fluency in English, was hard evidence that she had assimilated. She was someone who had accepted the "patchwork quilt" of America.

And yet, long after she received her American passport, she still called Indian associates, waiters, and friends kalas behind their backs. This term was usually said with a discreet smile, as if she was being simply mischievous. The family excused her, in most cases pleading ignorance. Or we dismissed it as a Burmese habit rather than indicative of some deep-seated racism. My mother, more aware of how inappropriate it was, would shush my grandmother in Burmese every time, while my uncle would scowl and let out a disapproving bark. But it never stopped her, really. I had found, whether I liked it or not, another complication in the family narrative.

Remembering my grandmother's awkward behavior reminded me of something urban liberal white folks discussed every year: the trip back home for the holidays. An "enlightened" white friend's beloved uncle or grandparent would let loose a racial insult over dessert, poisoning the atmosphere. It was not easily laughed about, because that kind of racism—white racism against black people, immigrants, or Jews—was connected to the worst of American and Western history, to pogroms, to slavery and lynching, to genocide. For some reason my grandmother's vague slurring of Indians seemed more embarrassing than genuinely disturbing. Until I examined it a little more closely.

Her general predisposition toward Indians as untrustworthy outsiders, a race to be skeptical of, became even less acceptable once I looked at the blood-soaked history of Burmese intolerance. In trying to better understand Burma and race, and just how offensive the word *kala* might have been, I picked up *The Indian Minority in Burma* by N. R. Chakravarti. Written with a highly critical eye toward the Burmese, the book outlines fifty years of subjugation and violent oppression of the Indians at the hands of the Burmese—and it made me realize that my grandmother's casual-seeming bigotry definitely had sinister roots.

Some context: There were a lot of Indians in Burma when my family arrived in Rangoon in the 1930s. A whole lot more than I realized. Rangoon, in fact, had become a mostly Indian city. I didn't know this, because in her recollections, my grandmother never once discussed the city or its people. She always spent much more time on her comfortable world of teatime bananas and English-language newspapers.

For many years, it was assumed that Burma would become a Chinese state. But instead, it was the Indians who effectively colonized their fellow colonized. Here's how it went down:

In 1872, Indians were 16 percent of Rangoon residents. By 1901, they were 50 percent. Burmans made up only 33 percent of the city.[10] Indians were propelled back home by poverty, and encouraged to migrate over the border by immigration policy. The native-born Burmese population was angered about the lack of protections for themselves *and* wanted to punish the newly arrived Indians. Meanwhile, Indians were migrating in vast numbers: In 1922, 360,000 arrived in Burma. By the 1930s, Indians owned the capital city: They built Rangoon; they ran its businesses and they conducted its trade. The Indian chettiars already had a monopoly on moneylending, and played a big role in the agricultural field, but they dominated the trade and banking industries, too.

Though some were wealthy, the majority of Indians were Burma's laboring class. They harvested crops; they mined silver and lead; they ran ships up and down the Irrawaddy. They tailored suits and made dresses. And they were employed as house help—including that cook who worked for our family.

This Indian laboring class got little respect or security. Many were brought over the border at the Bay of Bengal under the guidance of paid smugglers (sort of like *coyotes,* who are paid to guide migrants over the Mexico–United States border). The conditions for crossing the sea route to Burma were subhuman—and dangerous. The dark, dingy ships had filthy water, suffocating heat, and not nearly enough bathrooms for the number of passengers. It was squalid.

On land, upon leaving the ships, most Indian immigrants were forced to the very bottom of the food chain. They were paid horribly low wages and lived in hellish setups, crammed into disease-infested, flooding lodging houses. Opiate and alcohol addiction were common, and living conditions were often filthy.

I don't know whether our family's gifted curry maker lived in squalor, but the fact that many (if not most) of his countrymen and women did adds context to his stealing. Perhaps he wouldn't have had to if he—and people in his situation—were treated with more respect, or given access to better resources and fairer wages. And while the disappearance of baubles and gemstones was enough reason for dismissal from the family home, perhaps there were other forces that cemented his fate. Indians were regarded as inferior—my grandmother had no shame referring to them as kalas for the rest of her life.

I'd always presumed that we, my Burmese family, had been the oppressed: forced to flee our homeland to restart in America, a family of brown exiles who created a new life on Western shores. But as the reality of Burma's tortured history unfolded in my research, I realized that we outsiders were once insiders, perched atop an unsteady hierarchy. Turns out, we the marginalized had also once marginalized a whole class of our own—we'd just done it on the other side of the globe and left it out of the stories we told ourselves later.

Inevitably, this is true for families and their ancestors everywhere. So why pretend that these behaviors aren't part of *most* of our histories? Why tell one another and our children that back then it was just the golden oldies? History has no real beginning or ending; we simply choose points that are most convenient for the narrative—especially as it concerns the stories about our success. In other words, a whole lot gets left out.

CHAPTER FIVE

Even in Burma's peaceful days, the problems were the same as they are today: the powerful versus the powerless; tensions around immigration and labor and dark skin. How did a society react when faced with a wave of immigrants, people who were driving the economy of a country but were nonetheless treated miserably? By using shame and marginalization to keep these immigrants down.

The British Empire partly maintained its power by distracting its colonies with infighting. Their divide-and-conquer strategy planted the seed of hatred between the Indians and Burmese. When upper-class Indians fought for the British during the Anglo-Burmese wars, the Burmese deemed them the enemy. Until Burma formally separated from India in 1937, Indians often took the high-ranking positions in the British government of Burma, and the country's army was composed largely of Indian soldiers. In a 1938 pamphlet on Indo-Burman conflict, a young political leader named Thein Pe Myint put it bluntly: "When the British attacked and occupied Lower Burma as well as Upper Burma by unlawful force, their work was done mainly by the Indian Sepoys. For this reason, *we Burmese hate them*" (emphasis mine).[1] It turned out that a flimsy pamphlet would have a greater influence than expected.

Indian officials lived and drank and dined largely among themselves (or with the British), rather than with their Burmese peers, and therefore the relationship of immigrants in Burma to the middle- and upper-class Burmans—like my family, for example—was not one of solidarity, but of intrusion and of oppression. My grandfather U Myint Kaung may have gone to British schools and worked for the British monarchy, but he was still a Burmese Buddhist. He knew exactly who had conquered his country—and with what Indian assistance.

My family was still living in Mandalay when the Rangoon riots of 1930 began. It started with a fight at the docks between Burmese laborers and Indian dockworkers. Indian workers went on strike on May 8, 1930, pressing for fairer, higher wages from their employers. The (mostly British) firms that hired them would not meet their demand. Instead, the British opted to break the picket lines by hiring Burmese workers for lower wages. Seventeen days later, the shipping masters finally cut a deal with their Indian dockworkers by agreeing to four pence extra per head in daily wages. The Indians ended up paying for this small raise in blood.

The recently employed Burmese scabs, who'd filled the jobs as the Indian workers picketed, didn't appreciate being replaced once the strike was over. Keep in mind this was the beginning of the Great Depression. Burmese workers swarmed the streets of Rangoon with swords and iron bars and anything else to inflict pain, and for nearly three days, they targeted Indian workers and shops. Because Rangoon was an Indian city, not much of the city functioned during this time—no sanitation systems, few public services, and no business activity. It was referred to as a riot. Really, it was a rampage.[2]

In the end, there was no clear number of how many Indian people were murdered. Most estimates place the figure in the nebulous "hundreds" of deaths and "thousands" of injuries.[3] For these three days of terror, just two arrests seem to have been made. No help or compensation was given to the families of the slaughtered. Rangoon's Indians, who received no support or protection, mostly just hid, then shut their mouths and went about their business. They stayed in the city until India and Burma formally separated in 1937. It was then that Burma was made a separate, independent colony under the British crown.

But separation didn't stop the violence. Burma remained under British rule. Nationalism—the extreme feeling of superiority over other countries—was on the upswing. The Indian minority in Burma had few (if any) protections under the law, despite what had happened to them in the decade earlier. Now, their complicated history fighting the Burmese for the British—as well as existing class tension—made them prime targets for angry Burmese citizens.

My grandmother was just finishing her studies at the university in 1938 when the tension came to a head again, this time targeting Muslims. A small booklet, printed in 1931 by a Burmese Muslim named Shwe Hpi, was highly critical of the Buddhist priesthood. Almost no one had heard of Shwe Hpi or read his pamphlet that dared to criticize monks, but seven years later, as Burmese nationalism was growing increasingly popular, several nationalist papers picked up old excerpts and printed them for the public to read.[4]

Suddenly, Shwe Hpi's pamphlet took on enormous importance. Nationalist broadsheets such as *The New Light of Burma* and *New Burma* made the situation worse by printing Islamophobic editorials, prompting a wave of anti-Muslim bigotry.

A quick side note: If you didn't grow up in a predominantly Buddhist nation, or with a Buddhist parent, it's hard to grasp the role that monks play in society. In Burma, they are the embodiment of virtue and enlightenment. They are given the utmost respect. Recently, the rest of the world came to understand the importance of Burma's monks during the Saffron Revolution of 2007—named because of the saffron yellow–colored robes worn by the thousands of monks who protested the oppressive military regime that had (a) run their country into the ground and (b) put their elected leader under house arrest for more than a decade.

These monks meant business; they were men of action. That the military regime had cut them down and drove them into hiding in 2007 was not just an insult to democracy; it was a rejection of Burmese values. For exiles and citizens alike, the image of a military officer wielding a baton against a monk was a sign that things—already pretty awful—had reached rock bottom.

But back to 1938. That year, racism and religious prejudice reached a crisis point during a demonstration at the country's holiest Buddhist shrine: the Shwedagon Pagoda. Amid the pagoda's gold-leafed spires and tinkling bells, violent anti-immigrant speeches fired up an unruly mob of protesters. The mob descended the hill and launched an "indiscriminate attack on Indians . . . on a scale very much larger than that witnessed in 1930 and 1931, including cold-blooded murders, grievous hurts, looting, arson, etc."[5]

This period of violence stretched from July to September 1938 and was described as "a long period of horror" for Rangoon's Indians—one that, tragically, wounded or claimed the lives of thousands. Again, little was done in the wake of this bloodshed. The government response—even in India—consisted mostly of public outrage rather than actual demands or actions to protect the Indian people, who had built Rangoon and were now being crushed by racist rampages.

The Indian Legislative Assembly declared that its government—as well as the British and Burmese—had been criminally negligent in protecting Indians' interests in Burma. But the Burmese had no interest in curbing their nationalist movement, which fueled the chaos. In fact, the outrage in India over the violence in Burma had the effect of worsening *Burmese* tempers. Nationalists "considered it an uncalled-for interference in Burma's internal affairs and threatened to take retaliatory measures if the Indian agitation was not stopped."[6]

It was sickening. The rage and destruction. The wild-eyed nationalism. It was also familiar to anyone raised in the twentieth-century West. Why did we keep doing this to ourselves? I'd thought, or hoped, that Burma had been somehow different before its fall, exempt from the cruelties of the masses and the bloodiness of power. It was not.

And as I learned about all this from Mr. Chakravarti's little book, I began to wonder: Where was my family when Rangoon was being torn apart? How had no one ever mentioned this to me? Somehow the violent oppression of Indians in our own backyard never made it onto the family radar. And it wasn't like the Burmese public was in the dark about what was going on.

It wasn't just Mya Mya Gyi, or the rest of our family, who avoided mentioning this violence. It was like cultural amnesia: the Burmese had erased its treatment of the Indian people from collective memory. So much so that my grandmother—nearly seventy-five years later—still felt free to insult them, never once mentioning that many Indians in Burma had been subject to abuses and assaults too numerous to list. How weird it seemed, in retrospect, that she would focus on the loss of her rubies and delicious lamb curry, rather than this terrifying chapter of violence.

Soon enough, following Japanese occupation in World War II, much of Burma's Indian population fled the country. Those who remained were expelled in 1962—a not-surprising (though still foul and heartbreaking) decision on the part of the ruling military junta. For the most part, this forced exodus of Indians from Burma was documented as a chapter of great shame. There were too many Indian exiles who remembered all the things they had lost in departure—businesses, friends, lives. There was so much devastation in the wake of this expulsion that Rangoon was never the same again.

How swiftly the family stories dissolved from "bananas at teatime" to something much more complex and sad and violent. I felt foolish for believing in the simple elegance of my grandmother's stories, for not questioning what was going on mere blocks from their house on Shan Road. I had believed our family mythmaking. Was this any better than the tourists of the American South visiting old plantation houses, marveling at the china and the gowns and the sweeping staircases, never once glancing past the big house to the slave quarters?

All this historic information threw a wrench into the narrative of repression and exile that my family had been spinning for decades. I'd boasted throughout childhood about my grandmother's status as an activist, her passion for righteous causes, and her personal fight for democracy in Burma. But that fervent patriotism, it turned out, was linked to something grim: a sense of superiority for being wealthier, for being lighter-skinned. Ethnic nationalism.

Fast-forward to July 2013: Burmese prejudice against Muslims is once again in the headlines. *Time* magazine runs as its cover story a picture of the Buddhist monk Ashin Wirathu, who is called "The Face of Buddhist Terror." Wirathu is headquartered in Mandalay, in central Burma, and he is the head of a violent Buddhist movement against Muslims. The language he uses is basically torn from the pages of the Burmese nationalist papers of the 1930s:

> *"We are being harassed in every town, being ganged up on and bullied in every town,"* he said to the Guardian. *"In every town, there is a crude and savage Muslim majority."*[7]

And yet, Muslims account for only an estimated 5 percent of Burma's population. (Buddhists are the overwhelming majority at 90 percent.) Nonetheless, Wirathu's followers have tried shrinking that Muslim population through slaughter: One particularly gruesome rampage at a Muslim boarding school killed thirty-two students and four teachers. And the repression in Burma has not been limited to followers of Wirathu—Burma's Muslim Rohingya have lived for decades as landless, stateless citizens in the southwest Rakhine State. Many are forced to live in squalid camps and are unable to vote in elections to choose representatives who might rally for their rights and free them from this deplorable existence.

In 2012, after a Buddhist woman was raped by an allegedly Muslim assailant, the Burmese military exploded with violence in the name of large-scale revenge. They threw 140,000 Rohingya people into camps for internally displaced persons.[8] By 2016, the military was perpetrating an all-out assault against this Muslim minority. In one particularly brutal incursion, 1,500 Rohingya homes were burned. An estimated 65,000 Rohingya fled to Bangladesh at the end of the year, forced out by searing violence.

And by 2017, the Burmese government was engaged in what one top UN official called "a textbook example of ethnic cleansing,"[9] the mass murder of a people. Rohingya villages were being burned, their residents raped, killed, and otherwise hunted. The cruelty the Burmese inflicted on them was unthinkable: Whole families were being extinguished, live grenades thrown through front doors. As a result, over 400,000 Rohingya fled Burma—desperate to survive.[10]

This systematic violence is often explained away as Burma's fight against the spread of Islam in Southeast Asia (Indonesia, Malaysia, Sri Lanka), countries that were formerly Buddhist territories. This is their mission to secure ancestral lands, or at the very least to act as a defense against a rising tide of violent extremism (never mind that they themselves are using horrific violence to do so). But isn't this really just Buddhists expressing long-held bigotry against Indian Muslims?

Most uncomfortably, I began to rethink my family's own brand of Burmese nationalism—which, okay, had nothing to do with violence, but was firmly rooted in the same nationalism as the movement that overthrew the British. My grandmother had long been a vocal advocate for Burmese democracy. She attended monthly protests and organizational meetings. She read news from the homefront fanatically. She held strong opinions about what was happening back there, reserving her most pronounced disgust for the military leaders who had destroyed her country beyond recognition. The actual battlefront may have been on the other side of the world, but she considered herself a soldier nonetheless.

The leader of this pro-democracy movement, the spiritual guide in both Burma and abroad, was (and is) a woman named Aung San Suu Kyi. She is the daughter of Aung San, a nationalist Burmese icon, who led the Burmese in the struggle for independence from the British, and who was assassinated shortly after. From birth, Aung San Suu Kyi has been an object of fascination to

all Burmese, given her lineage. After the 1988 uprising, when the military junta seized power, she took on
almost mythic qualities. Witnessing the events unfold
around her, she became a leader of the resistance, making
speeches and writing what would become the most important texts in the pro-democracy movement.

She was subsequently placed under house arrest,
where she won the Nobel Peace Prize in 1990, though
she never accepted it. Knowing she would be denied
entry back into the country if she ever left, Aung San Suu
Kyi opted to stay in Burma, resolute. She made the decision to leave her young sons and husband behind in the
West, because in this struggle, she understood herself to
be more than a woman, a wife, a mother: She represented
the hope of freedom for the Burmese people.

Aung San Suu Kyi's democracy, born from the independence politics and nationalism of her father, was the
accepted standard in our household. And we all simply
assumed that because the military dictatorship was so impossibly villainous, the woman who resisted them must
be on the right side of history instead.

But what of her ties to Burmese nationalism—the
same kind of Burmese nationalism that has been embraced by villainous military dictators? Aung San, her father, had been assassinated just as Burma was coming into
its own, when his leadership might have been put to the

test. He had been the nationalist movement's hero. He led negotiations with the British to return Burma to its rightful owners—the Burmese. But noble as that contribution was, Aung San's political associates were also key players in that ugly chapter of 1938 in which scores of Indians were targeted and killed. Aung San himself may not have been a xenophobic murderer, but he *was* a supporter of Thein Pe's pamphlet, the one that made no secret of the thorough disgust Burmese felt for the Indians.

The pamphlets and speeches from the time were racist—case studies in Us versus Them. And the sentiments expressed in them were embraced by Aung San, the leader of Burma's revolution, the hero who everyone in my family admired, the guy I'd known about for as long as I could remember, the father of the freedom-fighting woman whom my grandmother had rallied for, all those Sundays on the hot pavement outside of the Burmese embassy in Washington, D.C.

Following Burmese independence, Aung San was assassinated. Burmese nationalists continued their campaigns, expelling the Jewish Baghdadis and Parsis and all remaining Indians from Rangoon and Mandalay. Internationalism was effectively erased, and businesses, banks, schools all were forced to adapt. Nationalism basically shut the country down and stole its sunlight. The movement also reengaged one of the world's longest-running civil wars within the ethnic tribes. Yes, the British were blamed for Burma's near century of misfortune, but what about the Burmese who pushed so many out?

This dangerous and deadly time did not end when the military junta eventually surrendered much of its power to a democratically elected government. Aung San's daughter, the very same icon my grandmother had championed, was now, decades later, turning a blind eye to the organized execution and persecution of her fellow countrymen, the Rohingya. Aung San Suu Kyi, now in control of Burma's government, reacted defiantly when faced with news reports that the Rohingya were being targeted and were fleeing the country in staggering numbers. She pointed to attacks launched on Burmese police outposts in the region by an armed local group calling itself the Arakan Rohingya Salvation Army (ARSA). It was a tiny group, but she labeled their attacks as "acts of terrorism." Was this the justification for a military response against the Rohingya that displaced nearly half a million people? Was this the same woman who had been held up as a paragon of justice and human rights just a few years prior?

Aung San Suu Kyi may have been out of touch with the international community as far as the Rohingya were concerned, but she was apparently very much still in favor with her fellow Burmese. Many agreed with her and supported her disinterest in protecting Rohingya Muslims from violence. Buddhist nationalism was still hopelessly intertwined with the religious and ethnic hatred that had plagued Burma when her father was alive. No one knew any better than they had nearly a century ago.

My grandmother placed herself at the center of the exiled pro-democracy movement, rallying for the release of Aung San Suu Kyi from her house arrest. "Those *people!*" she would say, in reference to those she saw as bringing on Burma's decline, too angry or frustrated to summon an adjective to describe their evil, their incompetence.

I had always assumed we were in no way implicated in Burma's destruction, its brutal killings. We had left; therefore, we were excused from examining whether we, too, might have harbored some of the same exclusionary, misguided ideas about Burman superiority—the delusion that allowed a Nobel Laureate to look the other way when ethnic cleansing was happening in her backyard. That sort of behavior had always been understood to be someone *else's* and not ours, despite the fact that those beliefs helped shape our identity—the very identity I was so eager to explore and celebrate, to reawaken in my own life.

We wanted to believe that we were different from those who'd stayed behind: Burma was crushed, fossilizing, broken . . . but we were not. Our family remembered when Burma was the rice bowl of Asia, but not what we had embraced that brought about its decline. Instead, we mourned the glorious past and longed for it once again. Easy to say from the other side of the planet.

When I'd begun peeking into the spaces between the stories I'd been told, what I discovered . . . was turmoil. My grandmother's refined background disguised real problems: deep-seated racism and prejudice, violence, and economic disaster. Not just Burma's, but our own. Aung San Suu Kyi, whose radiant face decorated mugs and T-shirts and key chains, had turned out to be a fraud. For me, this discovery was like looking in a treasure chest only to find dust and ashes. It was the first time it occurred to me that the stories we had told ourselves—and indeed believed—were just that: stories. The truth, as it turns out, was complex, but more than that, it was fractured, like a stained-glass window that had shattered into tiny pieces and was nearly impossible to put back together.

CHAPTER SIX

Here's the thing about discovering skeletons in your closet: it's hard to put them back in there once they're out. For me, the revelations about my family history made it clear that I needed to go back to the source of the conflict and confusion. I needed to go to Burma.

I had a very specific mission in mind. I was going for my mother's birth certificate, written—as family lore would have it—on a palm leaf, per Buddhist tradition, left somewhere in the Burmese archives. I wanted to give my mother a piece of home.

The last time my mother and I had visited Burma, in 2008, she didn't recognize what had happened to her city. All those memories she'd had—the frangipani blossoms and palm leaf umbrellas—seemed to have vanished against the poverty and broken sidewalks. I couldn't imagine how strange it must have been for her to come home and feel like a stranger. When I returned to Burma for my family research, I found some relief in knowing that a new and quasi-democratically elected government was to be installed in Parliament—the first in over half a century—and the United States had begun reopening trade relations. Political prisoners were being released. Things, maybe, were looking up.

My plan was to find her birth certificate, but I was also going to Burma in search of some magnificent and mysterious personal connection. So much of my research into both Burmese history and our family history had left me feeling adrift and confused. I would try one more time to connect to my heritage via the land itself. I would go there, set foot on the soil, breathe the air, and experience a life so different from my American one that it would surely force some sort of epic revelation, some meaningful intimacy, some sense of belonging—even if it was complicated. Right? I mean, that was my intention, at least.

I was not alone in my decision to make a voyage to explore my heritage. All over the world, second- and third-generation immigrants return to their ancestral homes to see the ghosts of relatives come alive through tours of homes, monuments, cemeteries, and castles.

In Ireland, you could tour the fifteenth-century Bun-ratty Castle for a keener, more tactile understanding of your family's left-behind history. Or you might hop a flight to Accra and come face to face with the slave traumas of Ghana's past, traveling along the 156-mile southern coastline, where the crumbling castles and forts still echoed with the terrors of the 1700s. There was something particular in the land, something that made the past come alive when you put your foot to the ground in the hopes of discovering something meaningful or clarifying. Heritage travel, as it is called, might not just be for reminiscing about the long, long ago: Perhaps it would be equally as useful to recall the recent past.

And so: First, I intended to hunt down evidence that we had once lived there. I wanted to see the old family homes, imagine my grandfather puffing on a cigarette and making the decision to leave for America under cover of night. I also wanted to see the teak palace in Mandalay where my great-great-grandmother once served in the shadow of the king—even if by now, the palace was just a re-created version.

There were so few photographs or heirlooms that survived our departure from Burma that it was sometimes hard to believe those times had ever *really* happened—from the metal containers full of vindaloo to the English-style garden parties. Everything about Burma was hidden beneath a sheet of distance and loss, like a famous shipwreck that everyone talked about but no one could find. Here was my chance to find whatever was left.

I wanted to see the things that had remained there after we'd left. I wanted to touch things that were permanently Burmese, things my relatives would have touched, too. This was, of course, going to be close to impossible, because Burma's official records and archives were sort of like a sand castle: damaged and frequently destroyed.

I knew that the place I would need to visit was the National Archives of Myanmar, but gaining access to that building would require an unreasonable amount of office administration and paperwork. A Google search showed that any requests for entry had to be accompanied by a letter, sent to the Burmese embassy, detailing very specifically what you were researching and why. It might take weeks to get a reply, if you got one at all.

My New York City–based book editor signed an official-seeming request on letterhead, confirming that I was working on a book and would need access to records pertaining to "Myanmar history and social development." I decided I would need backup in this mission (especially because I couldn't speak or read a word of Burmese, apart from questionable kitchen lingo pertaining to dried shrimp and fried summer squash), so I brought along my

Burmese-speaking cousin Geoff. He was working on his PhD and therefore had oceans of time to spend in libraries. I hoped his impressive-sounding status as a doctoral candidate at Columbia University might help us win over the authorities.

We received nothing in the way of response from the Burmese embassy in Washington, D.C. I decided not to let this discourage us. I believed myself to be persuasive—especially face to face. What if Cousin Geoff and I just tried to talk our way into the archives? We decided to go for it. After arriving in Rangoon, Geoff and I got to work contacting anyone who might have even the slightest knowledge about how to gain access to the building.

To help us navigate the process, Geoff suggested we enlist his former Burmese language tutor, a sassy woman named Yu Yu, who had assisted a number of Americans during their travels around Burma. Yu Yu introduced us to a French scholar who'd gone through the process, who, in turn, advised us to go to the office of a very famous Burmese academic and request a letter of recommendation from him. Visit a man who had never met us and had no idea what we were doing in Rangoon? As far-fetched as this sounded, it was apparently something he was accustomed to doing, the Burmese way of things that we were not yet accustomed to. Yu Yu got in touch with him, and we meekly asked him for the letters. The academic could not have been less concerned, or surprised, about the strangers at his door and signed our letters in short order. We were on our way.

The archives were located on a drowsy residential street and were far less intimidating than I had imagined. Most of the Burmese government buildings I'd passed by were hulking, turn-of-the-century stone constructions built by the English as if to withstand a world war (and they did, for the most part). Relieved to have made it this far, Geoff and I practically skipped through the main gate to the archives building, convinced that we belonged.

Our lightheartedness dissipated slightly when we were ushered into a second-floor waiting room that had the unnerving air of an interrogation room. Geoff and I waited quietly, unsure about what was to come. Despite whatever connection I had to the country, the unpredictable nature of Burmese bureaucracy made me feel like I might get deported at any minute. The deputy director general of the National Archives of Myanmar, a heavyset man in uniform, entered the room to review our paperwork. He then demanded to see the recommendation letter from my editor.

Of course, at this point, my editor's signed letter, the one that vouched for my character, was lying on the desk of some administrator at the Burmese embassy in Washington, D.C., useless to me in Rangoon. All I had on hand—in the car out front—was an unsigned printout of a Word document. It didn't look very convincing. I excused myself from the room so I could run back to the car and huddle in the back seat and fake my editor's signature on the letter, hoping that the ink would dry in the time it took me to return to the deputy director general's office.

I handed the letter over to the deputy, wincing at my obvious forgery and noting that my editor's "signature" bore no resemblance to his actual name. But given the many improvisations I had made to get here, my gut said that this would not necessarily be an issue. Once the deputy director general gathered all our application materials in a cardboard folder, he disappeared once again for an extended period, during which Geoff and I exchanged nervous glances.

"What do you think he's doing?" I asked in a whisper.

"I don't know!" Geoff replied.

To our great satisfaction, the deputy returned with approval. He said that if we desired any records between the years 1963 and 1965, the request would have to be assessed through an official request, and approved (or not) accordingly. Those were some of the most fraught years in Burma's struggle after gaining independence. The government seized and consolidated power, nationalizing the economy, expelling foreigners, and otherwise laying the foundation for the country's swift decline. It was no surprise that those years were off-limits.

Those years were also, of course, the most critical ones in my family history, I thought with a frown; 1965 was the year we finally left Burma for the United States, and I wanted to read about it. My grandfather had felt the hand of the government clamping down and realized that if there was to be a future for his children, it would not be in their birth country.

I would take what I could get, though. First, we were asked to sign a guestbook with our personal information. Then we were required to complete a two-page application asking for pretty much the same information. And then we were told to compose a handwritten letter addressed to the director general—once again, saying much the same thing. The woman who was helping us complete this secondary application informed us that we would need to present our passports, as well as two passport-sized photographs.

A day later, passport-sized photos in hand, we were finally allowed entry to the archives and granted full research privileges (except for those crucial years of 1963 through 1965), which was both exhilarating . . . and a complete letdown. I was looking for birth records, property records, government records—any official documents, really—but it quickly became clear how limited the record collections were. So little had been kept. It was as if Burma's history since independence in 1948 had been nearly wiped away.

Finding those birth certificates was a pipe dream. If my mother's palm leaf had ever existed, it had been lost long ago. Records of who owned property were nearly unsearchable, and you could forget about any census documents. The British kept organized records of their *own* white citizens who were living in Burma and India—but they didn't bother to record the births or deaths or marriages of anyone who wasn't a Brit by blood. England may have been the ruling colonial power, but unless you were from the country itself, you were not the concern of official record.

I could find some random records. Among these seemingly dull documents I found something that mattered to me: a page from my own family's story. It was a booklet of rules for the state scholars program—a government program that allowed the most promising young Burmese the chance to study abroad.

One of my mother's cousins, a young man named Maung Aung Lay, had been a state scholar. Tragically, he died in a plane crash on his way out of Burma, bound for the University of Chicago as a physics scholar. My mother could vividly remember learning of the news of his death; she had been staying with her aunt Yee Yee and uncle U Thein Han at the time. They were Maung Aung Lay's parents.

"I would always sleep with my aunt," she explained. "And when she got out of bed, I'm sure I followed her. I remember that she and my uncle were listening to the radio that morning, one of those funny old wood and cloth-covered things. It was rectangular, and it stood on a bookcase in their living room. They were so intently listening to the radio that I'm not sure they knew I was with them. My aunt had her ear close to it, because I gather they didn't want to turn it on, really. I knew something was wrong—there was something very troubling and ominous about this radio listening, especially at that hour. It was dark, after all; why would they be listening so carefully to the radio?

"The next thing I remember was that there was a lot of hushed talk and weird crying sounds coming from the bedroom. I don't remember any news coming to me afterward—basically I sort of put it together. But I don't remember a scene where I found out."

Maung Aung Lay had left for America a few days

before. He flew from Rangoon to India, and his plane went down upon takeoff from India, heading west.

My mother had told me this story countless times, and it always struck me as both eerie and tragic. The bright future Maung Aung Lay had ahead of him, and the terrible end he met just as he was starting this new life—but also that scene back at home, with the radio in the early morning darkness. My mother couldn't remember much of the aftermath, but it clearly haunted her for the rest of her life.

For me, reading the rules of the program that ultimately took him away from us was a way to get a little closer to him, however indirectly. I wanted to envision his application, feel his anticipation as he left home for the first time.

The pamphlet showed that as a state scholar, my cousin had faced a rigorous physical exam prior to departure, one that checked for all the diseases of the era, with very specific questions. I laughed through most of these rules, but they managed to convey an impression that the world, at that moment, was a huge, disconnected place. Sixty-five years ago, before the age of the internet and easy air travel, the crossing of borders and commingling of cultures was a deeply serious thing.

I could imagine my cousin poring over this little rule

book, a preview of his new life. For a moment, sitting in the archives reading room, I felt a tingle of the dread and excitement that he must have felt, knowing that the world would never be the same for him again.

My grandfather's story was also reflected in this booklet. He oversaw the state scholars program during a short time working at the Burmese embassy in Washington, D.C., in 1956. At that point in his long career as a Burmese bureaucrat, he was the undersecretary for education. He also had personal experience with studying abroad: in 1951, my grandmother and grandfather had both been awarded Fulbright scholarships to study in the States.

According to my grandmother, they took Trans World Airlines to Bombay and stopped for a week in Paris. She recalled that they stayed at the Hotel du Lys on the Rue Serpente, and that she immediately fell in love with French coffee and croissants.

In this curious new city, my grandmother had been fearless. "I wore Burmese dress," she explained, "but saw Parisian ladies in their spring coats and went and bought a short coat in green at the Galeries Lafayette. They had perfumes and colognes there, and I bought a bottle."

Next, they flew into New York and took the train to Washington, D.C. My grandmother was off to study for a few months at Kansas State Teachers College in Pittsburg, Kansas. That was followed by a brutal winter at the International House at the University of Chicago ("I liked it because I could get good Chinese food!" she said), and then it was on to Augusta, Maine, where she tried skiing and chicken noodle soup for the first time. My grandfather, meanwhile, was completing his graduate studies at Indiana University.

How strange it must have been to live in Augusta or Indianapolis, coming from the leafy delta of Rangoon as my grandparents had. The village elders told my grandmother that when she was growing up in the tiny, dusty town of Pakokku, she used to always say, "When I grow old, I'm going to America." My grandmother couldn't remember where this desire came from, but she insisted it was true. And the elders of her village were sure she would, even then. She recounted their conversations: "Mya, you know, she was always talking about going as a child."

I asked my grandmother if it was hard when she finally arrived in America. In those long, cold months in the middle of nowhere, did she miss home? "Oh," she said, "there was no time to miss Burma." During those six months, she never wrote home or called her children— not once. I'd always thought assimilation was an act of bravery that required self-sacrifice and a strong heart. But my grandmother suggested you had to be a certain kind of ruthless, too.

From the period when my grandparents were stationed at the Burmese embassy in Washington, D.C., communications revealed nothing particularly informative. That seemed a little odd. After all, in the late 1950s and '60s, the United States government was trying to smother the spread of communism around the world using brute force. America's apparent goal regarding Burma was to ensure that it not turn into another Vietnam (a country the United States would invade in 1964, despite vehement protests). But you wouldn't have known from the archive's cache of cables (at least the ones that I had access to) that fanatical anti-communism—flames America fueled—had made its way up the delta to Rangoon.

My grandmother knew this, and her life was, in some ways, shaped by it. After she and my grandfather returned from that year abroad and before they left Burma for the last time in 1965, my grandmother worked as the head librarian at the U.S. Information Service library at the American embassy in Rangoon. She revealed that she'd first gotten the job because another librarian was suspected of having communist ties. This woman's husband had been targeted as a possible communist sympathizer, and his wife was fired. And so my grandmother stepped in. It was not a point of family pride that she had gladly taken a post vacated through a witch hunt against her colleagues—you wonder what she would have done if she'd been called before the House Un-American Activities Committee, the group that spied on and interrogated people with perceived communist ties, and frequently destroyed their careers and personal lives. But it was her posting at the USIS library that eventually led the U.S. State Department to get our family out of Burma after the government fell.

After General Ne Win regained power in Burma in a bloodless coup in 1962 and established totalitarian rule in the country (he had previously been the prime minister from 1958 to 1960), the westernized Burmese—especially officials who had served in the previous government (like my grandfather)—were eyed with suspicion. My grandfather was soon demoted to the post of a high school principal as punishment. Shortly thereafter, my mother took French lessons, and a government representative made clear that this sort of thing was *not* permitted: Burma was returning to its roots, the government insisted. Foreign languages and interests were not tolerated. Universities were closing and the economy was suffering. It was growing clearer that the life my grandparents had had in Burma was no longer possible. At the same time, the Library of Congress in America needed an expert on the Pali language, and here was Mya Mya Gyi—available and ready to move. Taking that post at the USIS library several years prior was, in the end, a move worth making for my grandmother. And so they looked to America as their next (and final) destination.

I had been hunting for a paper trail that would lead me back to my people, something I could touch with my own hands—whether a birth certificate or land deed—that would prompt a revelation about my heritage, but I was not going to find it in these archives. The elements had washed our particular sand castle away.

I was annoyed, but ultimately, I suppose I wasn't all that surprised. Did I really think a military junta that had driven the country's economy into the ground, shuttered universities, and otherwise prevented the free exchange of ideas and conversation would take the care to preserve records of what they'd done?

Disappointed as I was, I'd also seen glimpses of the family story—my story—in at least a handful of documents tucked away in the Burmese archives. And in those moments, I felt some small vibration of familial recognition—the thing I'd come halfway around the world hoping and searching for. And I wanted more.

Fortunately, the archives weren't the only source of information.

Yu Yu told us about someone named U Aung Soe Min, an art dealer and collector who had amassed an impressive collection of primary Burmese documents, one of the best in Rangoon. One afternoon, Geoff and Yu Yu took me to his gallery, a maze of small rooms, each crowded with eight-foot-high stacks of newspapers, magazines, posters, documents, pamphlets, property titles, propaganda, and paintings. There was absolutely no organization to the collection, with records from the late 1800s stacked alongside pop culture from the 1960s. You had to be guided through each document—or stack of documents—by the man himself.

I wanted to know how U Aung had managed to obtain all this . . . stuff. It was like an alternative, secret archive. He explained that after the military took power in the late sixties and nationalized the country, most of Burma's libraries had been shuttered and destroyed. A few remained open for research projects. There were private libraries and collections, as well. "But in 1993 and 1994 and 1995," he explained, "everything was destroyed."

Those years in Burma were ones of tumult. The international community was calling for the release of Aung San Suu Kyi, the leader my grandmother so admired. The junta did not listen. It continued to arrest and jail political opposition figures and other pro-democracy reformists. And apparently, the crackdown was not limited to people.

"The libraries, the old books and documents, they were just on the streets. People sold them on the street," U Aung said. "I witnessed this. Archives of the Japanese occupation? On the street. Those valuable documents, research, interviews, collections of local history—both social and economic—were totally gone. [They] wanted to erase that history."

U Aung thought there might be private collectors interested in the material, and wisely started buying the documents from street-side book merchants.

"I wanted to start the most serious collection," he explained. "Most are not my interest, but they may be needed in the future. . . . It's very sad in Burma; the generations don't maintain their previous generation's work." For holding on to these items, U Aung had even been arrested. Collecting these artifacts from Burma's past was illegal, but I was grateful that he'd done it.

And so, piled up in his various rooms, I found . . . all sorts of things. There were political cartoons with a distinctly Burmese style, tone, and humor. They were sassy and unlike anything I'd seen before. There were happy-looking illustrated guidebooks to Burma's ethnic minority groups. There were pop-art pamphlets and cheeky photo illustrations of Burmese pinups. There wasn't a shred of evidence of my grandmother's Fulbright program, nor was there even a dim hope of finding my mother's birth certificate, but what I found in U Aung's collection was maybe, in a way, even more valuable.

The documents were sophisticated and funny and suggestive. Here was evidence of Burma's flourishing cultural and intellectual life. Here was comedy and irony in full color. Here were ways of writing and thinking about government and society that I could understand.

I'd never thought about Burma like this before. But looking at film stills from the prime of independent Burmese cinema, I could easily imagine what it might have been like to *be Burmese*. I hadn't ever thought about this in a practical way: not just identifying with Burma as an ethnic and historic designation, but actually living life *as a Burmese person*. With U Aung's collected material, I could now finally envision a Burmese life—just as I had lived an American life so far. I could see myself at revival and art house theaters, collecting vintage posters for my teenage bedroom or writing thinly disguised political manifestos for campus publications—just like I had growing up in the States, experimenting with vegetarianism and trying to develop an appreciation for films and books and art.

What I learned in this moment was that Burma wasn't all palm-leaf birth certificates and delicious *mohinga* noodles. I should have known that, of course—how stupid to assume otherwise—but I'd had no proof. So here was my discovery: I could now imagine a vivid interior life as someone who'd grown up in Rangoon rather than in Washington, D.C.

As exciting as this was, it also made me angry—because these piles of artifacts were just that: remnants of a golden era, an old worldview. Burma's particular brand of interesting and occasionally joyful cultural output seemed to have met the same fate as Burma's libraries: It had been tossed out on the street. At least as far as I could tell from my brief research in the homeland so far.

The only remnants I could find of this funny, freaky, hidden past was U Aung's haphazard collection, scraped together by one man who understood the loss. Did societies really unwind themselves like this? Could a culture that spoke fluently and with vivid language be silenced? It didn't seem possible, but here was proof that it was.

And, I wondered, who was at fault? What idea took hold that would burn a thriving culture and scatter its ashes? Was it the same force that was behind the slaughter of Muslims and the expulsion of Indians? The same menace that prevented my mother from improving her French and smeared my grandfather for his cosmopolitanism? The same power that insisted on nationalism as the ultimate virtue; that valued blood over every other form of identity? Could it be the same attention to blood and heritage that I was now embracing, if in a seemingly more innocent form—the force that had sent me hurtling back to Burma in the first place?

Maybe—but I wasn't ready to settle on that unfortunate conclusion yet. Instead, U Aung's words echoed in my head: "It's very sad in Burma; the generations don't maintain their previous generation's work."

CHAPTER SEVEN

With this cultural loss as my motivation, I was getting antsy to see as many artifacts as I could before they were tossed out on the street or destroyed or otherwise forgotten. At the top of my list were the old family homes, in the hopes of checking that they existed, proof that we'd really been here. This was my chance to savor a place linked to my past before it evaporated, too. Before I left for Burma, my grandmother had given me vague directions to her former house—guidance that wasn't much more than a trail of bread crumbs. "We lived across the street from St. Xavier's church," she had said, "and near my school, the Wesleyan Methodist mission school."

Armed with little more than this thin recollection, I flew from Rangoon to the ancient capital city of Bagan, and took a boat up the Irrawaddy River to Mandalay. Mandalay was where my grandmother had lived after her birth in Pakokku (near Bagan) until she was sixteen, when she and her parents left for Rangoon and all the glittery things the capital city had to offer. One of the only photos from her childhood shows a seven-year-old Mya Mya standing with her siblings and parents in the front yard of a large teak house, saluting her father in awkward fashion, possibly custom when it came to formal Burmese family portraiture.

I wanted to find that house, assuming it was still a house. I went to the neighborhood and walked around for a few blocks before stumbling upon the Wesleyan Methodist mission school. In the yard of the mission residence next door, the headmaster's daughter, a cheerful young woman named Gracie, came out to see who we were and offered to introduce us to her father, the Reverend Dr. Zaw Win Aung. The reverend later informed me, to my great disappointment, that the original church, mission school, and mission residence had all been destroyed during World War II. This did not bode well for our family house, which had been within blocks of all these buildings.

My great-great-grandmother, an attendant in the court of King Mindon Min, had purchased the home from one of the queens. The house, not surprisingly, was located on the outskirts of the palace compound, which was made of magnificent teak. After the British gained full control of the country in 1885 and the last Burmese king was exiled to India, the British took hold of the palace and renamed it Fort Dufferin. During World War II, both the Allies and the Japanese bombed Mandalay to smithereens. Almost nothing survived.

And yet, I walked and walked and walked that neighborhood, looking desperately for this house, even though the chances that it was still standing were slim to none. I'd look down at the old photograph taken from the front yard, then look up along the streets for anything even vaguely resembling that house. I was convinced, for whatever reason, that that house had to be standing, *somewhere;* that history couldn't keep disappointing me; that all of our time in this country hadn't simply turned to vapor and ash and dust.

And I think I found it.

Hidden behind laundry lines and fences, here was an old teak house on a corner, in roughly the right area, with a yard the right size to have once grown hollyhocks and jasmine. There could be no undeniable proof, of course. I had to make an independent decision to believe that this was our house—or to not believe it. All along, I'd thought this journey would offer definition and certainty. But what I was learning was that when it came to heritage, where it concerned identity, there was no guarantee of truth. In fact, I would have to decide—on my own—what was proof, what was an answer worth accepting. As with the house, I'd have to determine that I'd found what I was looking for: There was not going to be a finish line.

Back in Rangoon, I had general coordinates for my grandmother's first apartment in the city, the one that had running water and an English toilet. It was on East Fifty-Second Street, and it had been located "around the corner" from the post office. I found the post office, which was the same one that had stood in 1933, but all the apartments around it had been refaced or rebuilt.

I knew that I wouldn't be able to determine exactly which building had been hers, but I hoped that I'd see some façade or structure that looked like it *could* have been. Something that might allow me to imagine her and the family living there. But nothing gave off any sort of lingering scent of our Burmese history; nothing looked as if it had withstood the decades in between the last great war and the present day.

So the family homes themselves had been destroyed or were otherwise hidden. And yet there were still signs that would point back to the lives my grandmother and mother had lived in this place: institutions and buildings that housed more than just our family, but ones that could tell at least part of our history.

After my grandparents returned from their two-year embassy posting in Washington, D.C., my grandfather was made the undersecretary of education in the administration of Prime Minister U Nu, who governed the country before Ne Win. The prime minister was a well-intentioned but unfortunately ineffective leader. He was a contemporary of Aung San's, and he became a champion of democracy in the years following Burma's independence. But his leadership failed in bringing democracy to the country during a tumultuous time of civil war. When the military takeover ousted U Nu's government for Ne Win's rule in 1962, my grandfather was "demoted" (my mother's term). He went from working in the Department of Education to a position as headmaster of the former St. Paul's English High School in Rangoon, which had been renamed Basic Education High School No. 6.

Basic High No. 6 was a sprawling, Hogwarts-style academy where the children of the British, Burmese, Anglo-Burmese, and Anglo-Indian elite were schooled in preparation for their eventual leadership roles as captains of industry and government. My grandfather began his headmaster job in 1965. I returned with Geoff nearly fifty years later, to see what was left of the school.

As we walked toward the school, it was clear that time had laid a heavy hand on the place. Given what else was going on in the country, it wasn't so surprising that the building was shabby and in need of repair. Cobwebs and thick soot coated nearly every surface. Paint was peeling off the walls. Classroom furniture was rickety and mismatched. The part of the campus that was no longer in use looked like a sunken ship. Former classrooms were filled with stacks of broken chairs, outdated electronics, and piles of yellowing paper. Some of the athletic fields had been completely taken over by vines and weeds. A lot of it looked haunted.

But the school was open that day. So we found our way to the principal's office to see if U Thant Gyi, my grandfather, had somehow left his mark.

The principal introduced himself as Kyaw Kyaw Tun. He was enthused by our interest in the institution. But there was, he asserted, no trace of our grandfather U Thant Gyi. Geoff and I were skeptical—after all, U Thant Gyi was the first headmaster of the school when the government seized its reins in 1965. Surely there had been a mistake if there was no record of his legacy. Alas, only Wikipedia seemed to remember, on its list of the school's headmasters since nationalization. There, at the top, was my grandfather's name. But it was nowhere else.

Maybe this made sense: My grandfather had stayed in his role as headmaster for only one year, after all. The government wouldn't let him leave for America with his wife and children, so he'd stayed behind until he could find his own route back to the States. The Library of Congress had already guaranteed safe passage and a new American life for my mother and grandmother and my uncle; my grandfather was the last one who needed to find a way out. He emigrated in 1968 and never looked back.

But if I was being cynical, it was no coincidence that he'd been wiped from the record. He'd left Burma, and in return, he was a ghost (as far as public record was concerned). I thought about it and reasoned that my grandfather, one of the gentlest and most good-humored men on earth, would probably have laughed, or shrugged it off. They could have their broken-down Burmese public school; he got America. I—his American granddaughter—would have to satisfy myself with that.

Not content to give up the scavenger hunt, Geoff and I went to Rangoon University to find my grand-mother's old dorm at Inya Hall. We rolled up in a sputtering taxi to find that the university campus was landscaped and newly painted, a sharp contrast to the decaying high school where my grandfather had once worked. The whole dorm complex had been repainted a flat burnt sienna with gleaming white trim that made the building look brand-new. The marble floors had been polished, and sunlight was streaming in. I could almost see and hear what it must have been like to be a student at Rangoon University.

As much as all the broken chairs and moldy documents at Basic High No. 6 had been depressing, they had also illustrated Burma's struggles over the years. The disarray told a story; it illustrated the passage of time. Conversely, the rehabilitation at Inya Hall, spiffy as it was, seemed to erase the evidence that something chaotic and destructive had happened. The appearance that everything was *just as it's always been* seemed almost to be a kind of lie.

To me, seeing a place where time had ticked on—where repairs had been made and scuff marks removed—suggested that people had continued moving forward with their lives. For someone who was intent on revisiting the past, it almost felt like I'd been left behind—lost to some universe that no longer existed. It was . . . lonely.

If there was one place in the whole of Burma where history and tragedy lay largely untouched for half a century, it was the Secretariat building. This elaborate Victorian-style building functioned as the administrative headquarters of the British during the colonial era. It was also where the father of modern Burma, Aung San, was assassinated (along with six cabinet ministers) on the nineteenth of July in 1947, less than a year before the British Union Jack was lowered for the final time and the Burmese were—finally—granted control of their own country.

Aung San's death was an earth-shattering event, the gunshot that changed the course of a nation. (Imagine if Lincoln had been killed before the end of the Civil War.) When the military staged its coup in 1962, it closed off the Secretariat to the public. Security guards and packs of wild dogs deterred anyone trying to snoop. Word on the street was that the bullet holes were still in the wall of the council chamber, and that the room itself had been made into a shrine. But the rest of it—the cupolas and domes and wrought-iron staircases and parliamentary halls—had been locked away for fifty years, left to the elements and destroyed by cyclones and earthquakes. The Secretariat had become—through neglect and endless gossip—the place of legend, of ghost stories, of conspiracy theories.

Naturally, I wanted in. To see the room where Aung San had died; to examine this perfectly preserved vestige of Burmese history. And not just the country's history—our own. My mother emailed me while I was in Rangoon:

I vaguely remember visits to the Secretariat with Poh Poh [my mother's father] when I was very young. Distinctly remember walking that long passage, along the balustraded balcony. I don't know if Poh had his offices there, but the building was among the places that anchored our world.

It was a place that had anchored our world. Maybe it still could.

I set about trying to sort out who could get me in. I knew that a group called the Yangon Heritage Trust, run by a scholar and author named Thant Myint-U,* was working with the Burmese government to determine what, exactly, to do with the Secretariat building. It was in the style of colonial architecture, and was ready (according to the government) to be repurposed.

Thant Myint-U was gracious enough to meet with Geoff and me and school us in the history of Rangoon's extraordinary colonial buildings. He sent us on a walking tour with guides who revealed some of the city's most impressive gems. But as far as opening up the Secretariat, he was noncommittal. The last person to tour it had been

---

* Thant Myint-U was the grandson of Burmese diplomatic legend and former UN secretary-general U Thant. He had also written a few books about Burma, including *The River of Lost Footsteps,* that most every Burmese person had read or held an opinion about. Generally, he made me terrified about my own half-Burmese inadequacies regarding language, culture, and history.

President Barack Obama, and while Geoff and I were eager to present ourselves as very important cultural ambassadors, it was not exactly the same thing.

Ever persistent, I badgered, pleaded, and begged anyone I could in any position of authority. I *had* to visit that building before I left. I refused to give up—and eventually, I found someone who would let me in: Derek Mitchell, our American ambassador in Burma. Perhaps he took pity on me, or perhaps it was because he himself wanted to see the building again, but several days before the end of my sojourn in Rangoon, we gathered at the gates of the Secretariat a few minutes before twilight, and miraculously, we were let in.

In the magic hour, the building was startling in its scale—and deterioration. A story-high clock was stuck at eight o'clock, the numerals mostly missing. A family of pigeons was nesting below. Whole wings of the building had seen their roofs cave in, the windowpanes long since gone, as bats cruised through the hallways before the sun dropped. But around another corner, things would be largely intact, in need only of a good mopping. A Victorian-era staircase, with its massive curving metal frame and the ghost of a dome that once topped it, was like something from an ocean liner. Vast, empty rooms were everywhere.

Walking through the Secretariat was like a waking

dream, and not necessarily a good one—one of those anxiety dreams where you stroll through the halls of school, but everyone has already left for the summer and you've missed the final and now where are you? Lost. It was a sprawling, melancholy building, full of memories that weren't mine but were still too eerily present to ignore. I thought about my mother's stories about her father and could hear the shuffle of feet, the thrum of typewriters, the hustle of a government office readying itself for its next act. The sound of life, of busyness, felt as if it had just momentarily drifted away—but how?

I was lucky to be inside. When we finally got to the room where Aung San was assassinated, I was nearly hyperventilating with excitement. For so long I had known this man, or at least his legend.

If I couldn't retrieve my mother's birth certificate, if our family homes had been destroyed, here was something concrete that might bring me back to the thing I'd been looking for since I landed in Burma: a reflection of who I was, proof of my belonging. My outsized expectations about finding my identity had cooled. I no longer expected a huge realization that would knock me sideways. But I still hoped there could be *some* sort of resolution, where I could at last place myself in the context of these people, this land. Here was my last shot at finding myself in a national myth.

We took off our shoes, per Burmese custom, and stepped into the room. It was not what I had expected. The walls were covered in linoleum, apparently covering up the bullet holes—some of the only physical testimony to Burma's violent transition out of colonialism. At the front of the room were garishly blinking colored lights surrounding a shrine to Buddha. I nearly winced at the sight of all this, trying to imagine the same room in America. What we might do to "fix" something broken but still central to our history. No amount of imagination stretching could really convince me that anyone would ever put just *a little* putty over the crack on the Liberty Bell.

When I whispered this to my cousin Geoff, he replied, annoyed: Who was I to say what an appropriately historical treatment should be? To begin with, keeping the shot marks on display would have been tacky and gruesome, no? It wasn't as if we kept JFK's bullet-riddled car in the Smithsonian, after all. Wouldn't tourists prefer to see artifacts that weren't crumbling?

It was, in the end, somewhat devastating that all the things I'd hoped to find—echoes and shards of some life I'd wanted to connect to—had been lost or repainted or thrown out on the street or papered over. And yet, as we walked out of the building, I thought about what my mother had told me: This place had been our anchor.

Yes, it had been left to bats and dogs, but the Secretariat was still standing. I could take issue with the state of affairs across the board, but at least I'd seen these places, slid my hand down the same balustrade that my mother had as a little girl, hand in hand with her father.

The Wesleyan Methodist mission school of the 1920s no longer existed, but I'd put foot to ground in Mandalay, the city where my grandmother lost her first teeth and learned how to read. I never found my mother's birth certificate, and my grandmother's dorm hall had been repainted and replastered, and Aung San's bullet holes were no longer visible, but I had learned something about my heritage and my people and my relationship to both, which came as a surprise.

These were not aha moments, nor any tangible heritage recovery stuff I'd arrived in Burma hoping to experience. Connecting to my people was more complicated than having a series of meaningful encounters over noodles and tours of old homes, as it turned out. But after all the searching and seeking and pleading and sneaking around, I managed to get a glimpse of the past (our past!) in its most unlikely and unusual form. I had—however impossibly—felt the echoes of my family's history.

I still was going to be frustrated by parts of Burma's history, just as I had felt frustrated by our family history. I questioned decisions made by the Burmese people and thought—in many cases—that they were unwise ones. I felt confused. And now I wanted to go home, where my connection to place and people was unquestioned, where things were less heavy and less consumed by loss. And home, for me, was America.

I'd set foot where my people had lived and breathed and taught and fought—but it was like visiting a new planet. There was no recognition like the one you hear from those who've traveled to outer space—that moment when they spy Earth from above the atmosphere, peering through that tiny glass portal of the space shuttle and know, with 10,000 percent certainty: that's home, and that's where I belong.

Maybe, then, it was time to try the other side of my family tree, the all-American one whose more distant branches had lately grown knotted, the Catholic intertwined (maybe) with the Jewish.

I'd gone east. Now it was time to go west.

PART III

THE AMERICANS

CHAPTER EIGHT

I'd assumed that I could unwind my mother's immigrant story and return to her roots. I'd wanted to surround myself with Burmese culture and claim it for my own. I'd hoped I could scavenge the remains of the past and feel less lonely, more sure of my place in the world.

What I found, instead, was that by the end of the trip, I was ready for pizza. I was tired of trying to communicate in Burmese. I was fatigued and angry about the heat that made me lazy and exhausted. I sounded like a spoiled American brat—maybe because I was one.

Begrudgingly, I conceded that I was not American in the way my mother was American. She, unlike me, was Burmese first, and then she was American. She lived in the United States, and she was happy to, but she was, and would always be, Burmese first. I was not Burmese first, as much as I had hoped to be, as much as I hoped that my Burmese half might compensate for my confused whole. But even if I cared deeply about my mother's roots, I still couldn't muster a deep sense of identification with them.

Perhaps I had more in common with immigrants who'd gotten rid of their earlier selves and histories, and thought, "So what?" when it came to what their ancestors had left behind.

In other words, immigrants like my father's family.

Europeans who came to America were drawn to these shining shores in part for liberation. They were looking for the opportunity to become something different from what they'd been in the Old World; to shed the restrictions of the places they fled. Or that was the story, at least—because there were plenty of restrictions in the New World, too.

In the late nineteenth and early twentieth centuries especially, white Americans systematically excluded and harassed new immigrants from Europe: the German and Irish, the Southern Europeans, the Jews. They denied them housing, jobs, and opportunities. Left out in the margins, these immigrants formed their own communities. But over time, many were tossed into the great melting pot and made generically "American." Or, some might argue, specifically *white* American—an important label, as it would turn out. The point is, to gain all that America had to offer, European immigrants assimilated. But often one unfortunate side effect of joining the new can be forgetting the old. We, the children of this generation, are now keen to remember, desperate for clues that might lead us back to the very places our ancestors left behind.

My father's family had taken a few elements of their Irish Catholic heritage—the church, the cuisine—and held on to them in the New World, small keepsakes to organize their American identities. They told wistful stories about the old days. But that was about it, as far as family history was concerned. They assimilated. And in the process, those elements of their identity—religion, language, and culture—became "American."

I wondered what got lost in this process. In sanding down the cultural differences, something *must* have been forgotten or thrown away. I felt drawn to the thing that might be missing—the thing that might have pointed my family, and me, toward a deeper sense of self and community than an assimilated identity could ever offer.

I thought back to my aunt's comments. Were we really Jewish? I didn't have proof. It was time to start sleuthing around and bothering strangers for obscure information. Again.

Iowa, my father's birthplace, was like a Norman Rockwell painting featuring wholesome children and white picket fences. His portrait of home came down to three things: family, church, and community. It was a place where children carried hot baked potatoes in their hands to keep warm and full during wintertime, where the mailman (my grandfather) knew each and every home, where neighborhood children played stickball in the twilight hours of summer and sat down to home-cooked meals of steak and corn every week.

Our family weren't farmers, exactly, but, as my father told it, much of his home life revolved around food: the growing, harvesting, cooking, and eating of it. With six children, a stay-at-home mother, and only a mail carrier's salary to support them all, the family ate home-grown, home-cooked food nearly all the time.

In the sizable kitchen garden and orchard, they grew herbs and vegetables and fruits: dill and thyme, endive and cabbage and potatoes, peaches and apples. There was a summer kitchen where the food would be pickled and canned or made into jams. My grandmother made her own lard and fried doughnuts in it on Sunday. She baked her own pies and breads (store-bought bread was frowned upon). Meat came from the butcher, but even that was old-timey and personal: the butcher shop would call my grandmother about a pig that had just been slaughtered and ask if she might like some pork chops. In these retellings, stories that I grew up with and could recite like they were my own, you could smell the aromas wafting from the family dinner table . . . and they were delicious.

As for my great-grandfather Henry Wagner, the man who had brought the Wagner family name to the United States from the Old World, there was remarkably little to share. When I asked my father about Henry, he replied, "I have no memory of my grandfather at all. I'm not even sure I was alive when he was." The only memory he could recall about my great-grandmother—Henry's wife, Anna—was her death. "My father came home," my dad explained. "It was a cold day and his glasses were all steamed up. And he was crying."

From the evidence I'd heard so far, I imagined Henry Wagner as a sort of stern character. Photos showed he had a thatch of white hair and a do-not-mess-with-me mustache—the kind of facial hair that meant business.

When the Jewish Theory presented itself, I came up with a hypothesis that went like this: Perhaps Henry had had reason to flee the Old Country with only the savings he could carry in his pockets, driven by scandal or necessity or curiosity to the shores of America, where he started over, never once looking back. Perhaps he was a highly focused man who had no time for remorse or nostalgia, and when he arrived in a state filled with Christians, he decided to become one, too. Not because he was scared of being singled out or intimidated for his Judaism, but because to be Christian was to make a break with the old and assume full membership in the new. This theorizing of mine was based on little evidence—but this is the outline I drew for myself, eager to fill in details.

What my father did recall clearly was his grandparents' home. Henry was known as a businessman and "a merchant." He owned a local establishment on Main Street, Wagner's Bar and Grocery, a small market with an adjacent saloon. In the bar, my father reminisced, someone had painted a big mural of people toasting one another with steins of ale.

Henry and his wife lived in a "really big house." My father, not usually one to notice home décor, said that there were lace curtains and real silver for dining, fine plates and crystal glasses. A formal dining table, chairs, and—hanging on one wall—a portrait of Henry in bow tie and suit. "He was very dignified," said my father. "Henry and Anna were very European. . . . It never occurred to me that I was from the working class, or different from the banker."

My father had been shielded from the discomforts of class consciousness. He also hadn't had to think much about race. "There were no people of color in Lansing—none," he told me. "A handful of Native Americans were the most ethnic people in town. The only person of color I saw before college was the dry cleaner. [He] was an African American man, and I remember being sort of struck by it. He was an incredibly nice guy—and my mother liked him a lot. But we never talked about race." I raised an eyebrow when my father said this—I've found that it's always a little iffy when someone white finds the only person of color (a person in some sort of service position, no less) "incredibly nice."

In fact, he went out of his way to tell me that if Lansing had a persecuted population, it was people of German origins. They were thought of as enemies in the wake of the First and Second World Wars. With the start of the war, speaking German became taboo. "And there was also a very subtle anti-Catholicism. I used to think of myself as being a minority," my father added.

In this town, at this moment, my father would have me believe that the outcasts were more likely to be the German-speaking Catholics than people who are systematically persecuted around the world, like the only Jewish family or the single black guy cleaning laundry in their town. Could it have really been that way? Was he trying to say that his community wasn't implicated in the country's foundational racist crimes: slavery, Jim Crow, anti-Semitism? It seemed pretty unlikely.

After all, how could we have managed to secure all this—the bounty of America, with its peaches and doughnuts and freedom—without taking something away from someone? Did the universe simply act with kindness in the case of my father's family, granting gifts without consequences? My father explained Henry's choice of Iowa as his destination because "They were giving land away: forty acres if you could farm it. The land was free."

Here it was, the snag. The unseen "they." Who was this "they"? And how had "they" acquired the land to give away? I knew that Henry Wagner arrived in Iowa somewhere in the 1870s or '80s, but I had no idea what he found upon arrival. From my time in Burma, I had already learned that the most interesting (which is to say, complicating) truths were to be found in those snags. I set out to determine where, exactly, this land—the land my family lived on—came from.

Lansing, Iowa, is in the farthest northeast quadrant of the state, situated in Allamakee County. On the east, the county is bounded by the Mississippi River; to the north it's hemmed in by the state of Minnesota. An Iowa history book I consulted had a matter-of-fact explanation about how the area came to be settled by the Germans and Irish and Norwegians of the mid-nineteenth century: "Allamakee was long held as a peaceful hunting land over which hostile Indians pursued the chase without collisions. It

144

was given to the Winnebago Indians in 1833, when they were forced to surrender their Wisconsin homes."[1]

"Forced to surrender" didn't sound good—in fact, it sounded terrible, and so I began looking into histories about the Native Americans in Iowa to find out how the Winnebago ended up in Allamakee County and what happened to them once they got there.

"Manifest Destiny," the idea that white colonists were entitled, even supposed, to settle what is now this country's land was a popular idea at the time. With this in mind, they pushed farther and farther west in the early nineteenth century. An early promoter of Manifest Destiny was a populist, racist politician named Andrew Jackson, who would go on to become the seventh president of the United States. Jackson fought in the War of 1812 and was a prominent lawyer and a slave owner. As president, he was responsible for the forced removal and displacement of tens of thousands of Native Americans from their home soil. Even though Jackson had been greatly helped by the Cherokee at the Battle of Horseshoe Bend in 1814, he ordered the forced removal of fifteen thousand Cherokee from their ancestral lands east of the Mississippi so that white settlers could steal the land. In so doing, President Jackson disregarded a ruling from the U.S. Supreme Court that had confirmed Cherokee rule, and set a deadly standard for the treatment of Native Americans elsewhere in the country. The expulsion of these Cherokee—as well as other tribes of native peoples—and their long forced march westward was known as the Trail of Tears. Nearly four thousand Cherokee died along the way, overcome by disease, exhaustion, and starvation.

In 1829, under Jackson's guidance, the U.S. government forced several tribes[2] to sell their land—eight million acres—extending from the upper end of Rock Island, Illinois, to the mouth of the Mississippi. These are lands that are now known as Missouri, Iowa, and Minnesota.[3] Native people were expelled from their own ancestral homelands.

Here's a letter from Potawatomi chief Senacheewane to Jackson:

> *To go away from our home is hard. But to be driven off without any hopes of finding home again is hard to think of, and the thought is equal to death. You do not know, Father, our situation and if you did you would pity us, for these very same woods that once made our delight, have now become the woods of danger. The river where we once paddled our canoes uncontrolled, has now become the river of alarm and of blood. Several of my young men have been killed by your white children & nothing has been done to cover the dead.*

Father—we cannot go away. This is our land,
this is our home, we sooner die. Come Father, speak
to us, and we shall try to please you.
     May the great Spirit above give you health
and a long life . . .
          I speak for my people—who are many.[4]

The Winnebago Indians back then were known as the Ho-Chunk Nation, for *Hochungra,* meaning "People of the Big Voice." The Ho-Chunk were forced off their land for $540,000[5] to make way for miners who had their eyes on the territory—though that didn't put an end to hostilities.

Some groups of the Winnebago tribe bravely resisted. They took up arms to reclaim their land in the Black Hawk War of 1832. When they lost, the Winnebago were forced to give up remaining homeland in Wisconsin in exchange for "neutral ground" in Iowa (plus $270,000 in twenty-seven annual payments). This "neutral ground" was a forty-mile-wide "buffer zone," where the feds said the tribe would have protection from predatory settlers and other warring tribes. The government assured tribespeople that they would be relocated to "better lands" when those became available. (They never were.)[6]

That so-called neutral ground included what is now Allamakee County—and it was hardly neutral. The Winnebago were forced onto territory that was being battled over by the Sauk and Fox (also known by their tribal name, the Meskwaki) tribes, and their common enemy, the Sioux. The Winnebago were now people without a home, caught between warring factions, and unsafe in their new territory.

In 1837, tribal elders sent representatives to Washington, D.C., to make their case to get their land back. The representatives were told they couldn't leave Washington without signing a treaty—one that would give away the rest of the Winnebago lands. It didn't matter that these particular tribal signatures were meaningless, nor did it matter that the feds said they'd give the tribe eight years to pack up and move out. In the end, after pleading their case in Washington, D.C., the Winnebago were allowed only eight *months* to relocate. I thought of Senacheewane again: *"Father—we cannot go away. This is our land, this is our home, we sooner die."*

This chapter took a deadly toll. What happened to the Winnebago is what happened to the Cherokee and Seminole, the Choctaw and the Chickasaw. In 1829, the Winnebago were estimated to number 5,800. By 1837, smallpox had killed off nearly a quarter of them.[7] Less than two decades later, in 1855, the tribe numbered only 2,754. A quarter century of warring, negotiation, settlement, and expulsion had failed to yield any redemption for the People of the Big Voice.

Reduced in number, diseased in body, broken in heart and soul, the Winnebago, who whites saw as a threat to their westward expansion, had been violently contained. By 1846, the tribe was uprooted yet again, moved out of neutral ground and over to Minnesota. Not surprisingly, the first white settlements in Allamakee County were established somewhere around this time. The town of Lansing, where my great-grandfather would live, was claimed and settled in June 1848.

In 1862, in the middle of the Civil War, the Homestead Act was passed, which opened up the great expanse of the American West to white settlement. Allamakee County was no exception. If the fight to claim this land had been bloody and long, the process by which it was given away was, ironically, remarkably easy for most Americans (except, of course, native people, who weren't considered citizens until 1924). Even immigrants could claim their land, provided they pledged their allegiance to the United States.

Once the Homestead Act was passed, and once the Civil War was over, what did all this now-empty land mean for people who were slaves, now free? My father had mentioned the lone black dry cleaner in town—shouldn't there have been black-owned businesses sprouting up all over the Midwest, an area that was closed to slavery? Indeed, under the Homestead Act, and once the Civil War ended, former slaves were technically able to claim pieces of land for themselves. And with a Southern landscape where racism and violence remained common, no doubt the West seemed enticing. But to migrate hundreds or thousands of miles required resources and networks that many newly freedmen and -women didn't have—and so many were forced to stay put and work for those who had once enslaved them.

But there were other reasons that the American heartland remained so white: Southerners made it very hard for newly freed black folk to leave the region. The movement of former slaves to the Midwest was greatly complicated by racism.

The National Park Service oversees many of the records relating to the Homestead Act and details the various cruelties white Southerners used to keep black people from leaving the South during Reconstruction:

> Southern whites continued to oppose the exodus. . . .
> Many went to extreme measures to try to keep
> blacks from emigrating, including arrest and
> imprisonment on false charges and the old standby
> of raw, brute force. African-Americans suffered
> beatings and other forms of violence at the hands
> of whites desperate to keep them in the South.
> Though these typical forms of intimidation did not

really prevent many freed blacks from leaving, the
eventual refusal of steamship captains to pick them
up did.[8]

It was impossible to settle a new place if you weren't allowed to leave the old one.

When my father said the land was free, he hadn't thought about—or cared to know, particularly—the price that had been paid by others. All that free land wasn't really free, as it turned out.

Ultimately, I couldn't get away from the fact that we had accepted the notion that all this land-getting had been somehow easy, or miraculous, as if there were no strings attached. It wasn't as if I now expected Carl Wagner, Jr., to offer a family plot to the families of former slaves and Winnebago descendants, necessarily. But, in retrospect, the ho-hum narrative about our Iowa origin story seemed incomplete, if not lazy. It made me wonder what other self-serving stories were woven into our family history, ready to be unwound.

"A handful of Native Americans were the most ethnic people in town," my dad had said. What a wonder this was, his white Lansing, his monochromatic Main Street. "The only person of color I saw before college was the dry cleaner."

Well, there was a reason for that.

CHAPTER NINE

My great-grandfather on my father's side had taken on an almost mythic presence in my head. According to my father, he was intelligent and spoke several languages. He was a man of the merchant class who appreciated fine things, like crystal and lace. But what had been lost in the story of his assimilation? Where exactly did he come from in the Old World, and what did he do there? Why did he leave? How did he end up in northeastern Iowa, of all places? Why leave a comfortable existence in Luxembourg to move to the wilds of Allamakee County? Did he conceal his religion when he arrived in America?

It had become clear that things were more complex than the wholesome picture my father had painted of his family, with its homemade bread loaves and hopscotch

Saturdays. I was discovering through my research that our American origin story—and, for that matter, probably everyone's—was messy. My father's story—I'll nickname it the White Immigrant Origin Story (WIOS)—was a familiar one; most of my white friends had one. "We came from some European country, and my great-grandfather made a good, honest life, and now we live in America and have an Xbox."

This is what I'd grown up understanding. This was the family history in circulation when I went over to white friends' houses after school to eat sandwiches and see their apple pie upbringings. The WIOS may have been a harmless story during my childhood years, but I had come to realize that it has been a source of much destruction in American life. It is a story about virtue, freedom, fairness, opportunity, cheerful assimilation, and hard work. . . . And it is in many ways a lie.

Even after my most basic investigation, my own family's WIOS had collapsed. That experience drove home the truth: Almost no one achieves their success or secures their place in this country in purely honest, harmless fashion.

The typical WIOS is filled with vague, dismissive lines. Like my father's explanation for why his grandfather came here: "They were giving away land." Of course it wasn't that simple—someone a few years earlier had stolen it and killed the people who once lived on it and *then* given it away to someone else—and we had conveniently decided to gloss over that, because we had either forgotten or decided to omit the cruelties from our American success story. And because enough people agreed to the WIOS, enough people didn't ask questions or look under the rock; it didn't matter that the land was stolen and its people slaughtered. It didn't really matter how many brown folks and black folks raised an eyebrow or a hand or a fist in complaint or caution. Nor did it matter how many of those people asked for the very same things that defined the WIOS and were denied them—or worse.

The irony of all of this was that, in the end, the WIOS didn't even *really* benefit white Americans. All the erasing and revision eventually wore the story thin. And when the truth inevitably started to come out, however many years later, it became cause for shame and denial. Who wanted to be descended from the people who'd ousted the Winnebago? Who wanted to be the family of a former slave owner? Nobody, really. You couldn't find a new family, couldn't choose your own roots—and so, instead, you had to dig deeper into the mythmaking of the WIOS, double down on its fantastical origins: Once upon a time, things in America had been great, and simple, and pure—how else would we have made it?—and we need to get back to that time.

This belief in the fundamental goodness of one's own people and their superiority, their righteousness, and the notion that nothing immoral or rotten preceded them—it was intoxicating. The WIOS is, after all, foundational to the concept of white privilege—the benefits granted to people who sit at the top of the racial power grid. And we sometimes forget that *privilege feels good*—and unfortunately, a lot of people are tempted to forget certain truths or otherwise simplify the narrative to experience that advantage. But for all of our sakes—brown people, black people, white people—now seems like a good time to shatter the myth that anyone's origin story is born of only virtuous behavior and fortunate choices.

For me, this meant finding out as much as I could about whatever the Wagner clan might have forgotten. At the top of the list was the possibility of our ancestors having Jewish roots. A discovery here would confirm that there *was* indeed a lie at the heart of my family myth, that there was a complicated story about heritage within my seemingly white, Christian family.

Interviewing family members for their recollections of our possible Jewish heritage had been useful to a certain point. But I needed specific confirmation from some sort of authority. That meant documentary evidence, things like birth certificates and marriage licenses. Census data. I had been through endless papers in my travels to

Burma, looking for evidence about what we'd lost. That which I did find had been wholly unexpected, and had sent me off in a different direction altogether.

But I had faith that the paper trail in the West might be better preserved: For one thing, Western Europe hadn't fallen prey to a repressive military government that had destroyed records—as if in destroying evidence, they could rewrite history. Instead, Western Europe had fallen prey to a fascist dictator—Hitler—who had systematically destroyed whole countries. And yet, Europe's libraries had not been ransacked, pillaged, or left out on the streets. There were legendary research archives across the continent. And America's records of who had arrived here and when were still intact—as far as I knew. I had hope, however uninformed, that the records I was looking for had been preserved.

As much as I knew about Henry Wagner's place of arrival in northeastern Iowa, I had little information about the man himself, besides the fact that he apparently spoke several languages, including French, German, and Yiddish. When did he meet and marry his wife? Was his last name really Wagner? Would census forms from the Old World list his profession? Why did he leave the Old World to come to America? And then, of course, that central mystery: Was he Jewish?

The easiest place to start was Henry's arrival in the

United States. There would be an immigration record that would list his name, birth date, and birthplace, and from there I might trace his steps backward or forward. I knew I was looking for a Henry Wagner born in Luxembourg around 1849. My father had mentioned a helpful detail: Henry had been involved in the Franco-Prussian War, which took place from 1870 to 1871. So I reasoned he would have been in Luxembourg around that time and left for America afterward.

Searching through the online databases of immigrant arrivals to the United States, I came across several "Henry Wagner" characters. One—twenty-three years old at the time of arrival—landed at the port of New York in May 1869 on the SS *Paraguay,* entering not via Ellis Island (which hadn't yet opened) but at nearby Castle Garden, now known as Castle Clinton. Another Henry Wagner was described as a painter. Nothing about the stories I'd heard about *my* Henry Wagner had made him sound like a painter. Then again, who knew? The man was a mystery.

Another Henry Wagner arrived July 25, 1870, but apparently came from Prussia and had been born in Germany, which seemed to make him an unlikely candidate. But I couldn't dismiss him out of hand, because I soon learned that Luxembourgians were often listed by the U.S. government as German because they spoke German.

The immigration records online showed many Henry

Wagners who'd arrived in New York from Germany over the years in question. Some had their profession listed as "farmer"; others listed no profession, because in the end they were coming to America to *become* whatever they would be. They left from the ports of Boulogne-sur-Mer and Hamburg and Liverpool and Cherbourg and entered America mostly through the port of New York (though others entered through the ports of Philadelphia, Baltimore, Galveston, New Orleans, San Francisco, and Boston). They came in on ships named *Etruria* or *Phoenicia* or *Normannia,* hulking steamers operated by White Star and Cunard and Inman, with two or three coal stacks to power them through the one- or two-week voyages across thousands of miles of Atlantic Ocean.

There were so many Henry Wagners who (sort of) fit the bill that it was nearly overwhelming. But as confusing as this became for my research purposes, it was also beautiful in a weird way. The multitude of men with the same name, all coming to the same place to start a new life—or fleeing various and unnamed disasters.

If there were this many Henry Wagners in the passenger records of the late 1800s, I figured it would make sense to start looking for other records from later on in my great-grandfather's life, too.

Soon, I came across two documents that gave me pause. Among the digitized records available online was a naturalization certificate for a man named Henry Wagner dated March 1, 1886. I knew this had to be him because it had been signed in French Creek, Allamakee County, Iowa. There could be no other immigrant named Henry Wagner in a place that small at that time (right?).

I was surprised at the date: 1886, by all accounts, was a good fifteen years or so *after* Henry had first set foot in America.* After his first children had been born. And, presumably, after he had opened Wagner's Bar and Grocery on Main Street. To imagine him still a citizen of the Grand Duchy of Luxembourg—and possibly an undocumented immigrant in America!—for such a long period of time, during such formative years of our family history, complicated my conception of our American beginnings.

I read on. As it turns out, up until 1906, there was no formalized record keeping around immigration or the naturalization process. For the most part, the process of becoming an American was like this: would-be Americans had to have resided in the United States for at least five years, and in their home state for one. (These requirements increased and decreased through the decades, depending on the political climate of the day.) It wasn't until 1906 that the Bureau of Immigration and Naturalization was even created.

When they applied for citizenship, immigrants had

---

* The Franco-Prussian War ended in 1871.

160

to prove they met the residence requirements; they were asked to renounce loyalty to any foreign governments, pledge their loyalty to the United States, and take an oath. It did not seem like a particularly difficult process. Perhaps more interestingly, there was no apparent record that this pledging even took place. No deportation task forces were on the hunt for Luxembourgian immigrants living in America. There was no mandatory period in which immigrants had to file for citizenship; some did so as soon as they could, while others, like Henry Wagner, waited nearly fifteen years.[1]

The process of becoming American at this time might have appeared to be relatively open—except, of course, for non-European immigrants. Take the Chinese Exclusion Act of 1882, which barred anyone from China from even entering the country. Here was a piece of history that is disturbingly familiar to any twenty-first-century American, who's witnessed the government reject people in need of refuge because of their race and religion.

Henry Wagner's naturalization is a reminder that undocumented people from two or three generations ago were mostly white men and women. And American law enforcement, it seemed, was pretty relaxed about it.

Laying eyes on my great-grandfather's 130-year-old naturalization certificate was moving. It reminded me of the thing we constantly say but never seem to realize: we are a nation of outsiders. I always knew this as it concerned my mother's side, because her arrival story was never *not* with us. I was reminded of it by virtue of her very being: She was Burmese and then she became American, and you could see that history in her face, hear it in her voice, feel it in her view of the world. But I had never really understood that the same was true on my father's side. His whiteness, his American ordinariness, masked the fact that he, too, came from someplace else.

Henry Wagner and his white descendants were allowed to claim the title of "American" because somewhere along the way, the country had decided that white American outsiders, after a time, were not outsiders; they became, simply, Americans. But brown American outsiders were—and would always be—brown American outsiders. They could (eventually) be given the "American" title, but only in hyphenation: African-American, Burmese-American, Mexican-American, as if the hyphenation clarified that these people were not exactly *full* Americans.

When, for example, had I ever heard the Wagner family referred to as Luxembourger-Americans? Precisely never. And yet black people who had families here for centuries—some for long, hard centuries—before Henry Wagner arrived on this land would forever be known as

African-American. They were pushed into a lower place on the American power grid.

In this moment, it became clear to me (as obvious as this was, it was still illuminating) that any claim anyone—who wasn't a Native American—made to being a *true* American was a lie. To say that you were the "real" American and that an "outsider" was not wasn't immigration policy. It was a power grab. *Everyone* in this country was an outsider.

When I discovered that my great-grandfather was naturalized in 1886, I had my first important notch on the family timeline. Now I began to look for other, earlier milestones so I could start to plot out a story that explained this man. I wanted to shed some light on Henry Wagner's ethno-religious background: When (and how) exactly did he marry Anna Wagner? Could she have been Jewish, too? Was their marriage one of convenience? Was it religious? Where did it happen? In the Old World or the New?

My cousin Karl had mentioned that he thought Henry Wagner had taken his wife's name, in part to disguise his identity after the Franco-Prussian War. (Karl also believed Henry may have engaged in treasonous activity, but we'll get back to that.) I secretly thought that maybe Henry had taken his wife's name to disguise his true, Jewish background. I wanted to see what the records showed about their life together in order to glean information about their marriage and children.

I first found census records from 1880. In curlicued English script, they accounted for Henry Wagner, a self-described thirty-two-year-old farmer from Allamakee County, born of parents from Luxembourg and married to a twenty-two-year-old woman named Eva Wagner. I had always been told that my great-grandmother's name was Anna, but Eva seemed close enough. Perhaps Eva was her middle name. Or maybe—and more likely—her name had been inadvertently changed by the administrative official who took her name for the census. Perhaps this person had bad handwriting or bad hearing or just a lack of concern about honoring the correct spelling of a foreigner's name.

Anyway, I went with it, and did so because the math mostly fit: I knew Henry had been born roughly in 1848 or 1849. According to this census record, he and his wife had three children, a two-year-old son named Heinrich and two daughters: one-year-old Catharina and six-month-old Mary. And I knew from our family records that the eldest of my great-aunts and great-uncles were Henry, Catherine, and Mary. This was the Wagner clan.

Once I was able to pinpoint the names of a few key family members (Eva Wagner was known as Anna Wagner, Catharina as Catherine, and so forth) and establish a timeline to work with, I was able to narrow my search for other biographical documents, including, most important, a marriage license. It wasn't hard to find.

Dated April 4, 1877, Allamakee County records showed the wedding of Henry Wagner to Eva Wagner. It did nothing to point me in the direction of the Jewish Tribe. Henry and Eva/Anna had married officially in the state of Iowa, and with the blessing of the Catholic church—no synagogue in sight.

But weirdly, unlike so many other marriage records, this document did not list the bride by her maiden name. This might explain why my cousin Karl believed that Henry had changed his name to hers, perhaps to disguise his identity. Unless they had just been born with the same last name.

I knew I needed professional help to find out more. I found Anne Kenne at the University of St. Thomas in St. Paul, Minnesota, who was a university archivist and the head of the school's Special Collections department. She recommended a site called Luxroots.org. Who knew there was enough of a community of Luxembourger genealogists to warrant its own site?

Luxroots.org was effectively the internet equivalent

of the bargain bin: You were sure there was a treasure buried in there somewhere—something that might fit the bill for whatever you'd been searching for. In this case, that thing was a name: Jean Ensch. He appeared to be the Sherlock Holmes of Luxembourg. Ensch monitored the site and acted (as far as I could tell) as the wizard behind the country's genealogical forum.

Again, I sent an email into the unknown. Could Mr. Ensch help me in my search? I was looking for information about my great-grandfather Henry Wagner of Esch-sur-Alzette: specifically, whether he tried to change his name (or alter his identity) in the wake of the Franco-Prussian War. I crossed my fingers.

While I waited to hear back, I went to genealogy chat rooms where various self-styled ancestry experts are waiting to comment or reply to questions. I posted my query on one of the larger ancestry websites: I was looking for any records pertaining to a certain Henry Wagner, born circa 1849 in Esch-sur-Alzette, Luxembourg, and/or his marriage to Eva/Anna Wagner.

Someone from Aurora, Illinois, with the handle *chi1k* responded within four hours. *chi1k* found birth records on FamilySearch.org for someone named "Henri Wagener" who was born July 31, 1849, in Esch-sur-Alzette. Amid several lines of medieval Germanic script, I found the handwritten name "Heinrich." Henri and Heinrich are variations of the name Henry, so I read on.

chi1k, already the most useful and generous virtual stranger I'd ever come across, explained that Henry's mother was a twenty-two-year-old named Anne Wagener. As with "Anna" and "Eva," or "German" and "Luxembourgian," online genealogy research tips told me that "Wagener" could have eventually become "Wagner." The spelling was probably sanded down through the generations, especially when it came to immigrants who were both leaving so much behind and trying to assimilate into a new culture. Anne's father, Peter (also known as Pierre) Wagener, sixty-six, was the only other male name listed on the document. There was no record of a father for the newborn.

Meaning: Henry Wagner was a child of a single parent, out of wedlock. At this time, that would have been a really big deal.

According to *chi1k,* this piece of evidence, scrawled in the margin of the birth certificate, supported that point:

Michel Mueller of Grevenmacher and Marie Anna Wagener married in Esch-sur-Alzette on 28 Aug 1856 (making Henri a legitimate child of the couple).

chi1k then posted a census document from 1867, which showed Michel and Anna Mueller (formerly Wagener), and their son Henri Mueller.

By the year 1871, another Luxembourg census revealed that "Henri" was no longer living with Anna and Michel Mueller. He had already left Europe to sail across the Atlantic and was on his way to becoming *Henry Wagner*—an American.

CHAPTER TEN

As fantastically helpful as *chi1k* had been, I was slightly worried that I was too reliant on his (or her) reading of the paper. Who was this person? I could only imagine presenting news about our forefather to my dad and aunts, and then citing the source as someone named *chi1k*. They would likely frown and ask why I was putting my trust in an anonymous online stranger to rewrite our family history. I had some doubts, too.

Finally, the Luxembourgian expert Jean Ensch surfaced, like a submarine rising out of the dark sea at the least expected moment. He had checked the birth records of Esch-sur-Alzette and found the exact same one that *chi1k* had sent to me:

Peter Wagener declared that his daughter Anna
Maria Wagener, aged 22 years, had given birth
to an illegitimate child, whose given name was
Henry. A marginal note specifies that a recognition
of fatherhood and a legitimation by marriage was
performed at the marriage of Michael Muller and
the mother Anne Marie Wagner (spelling now
Wagner in marriage record), which occurred 28
Aug 1856 in Esch sur Alzette.

At that point, Henri Wagner became known as Henri
Mu(e)ller.

As Ensch put it:

The groom recognizes the fatherhood of the child
and allows that the child shall bear henceforth the
name of Muller and have all the rights attached to
the status of a legitimate child.

Knowing little about European social customs of the
mid-nineteenth century, I guessed that, at that time, having children out of wedlock was not exactly smiled upon.
My great-grandfather, who had fathered a Catholic clan
of thirteen children, must have kept his origin story a secret. These children, in turn, fathered a next generation
of Catholic sons and daughters who hadn't the faintest

inkling that their grandfather himself had been born out of wedlock. And then adopted! Had Henry also been covering up other biographical details—namely, ahem, Judaism? The introduction of Michael Muller would provide another branch of the family tree to explore as it pertained to "Our Jewish Roots."

Furthermore, for a time—at least from the age of seven until he left for America—he was known as "Heinrich Muller." It was unclear whether Henri Muller officially became Henry Wagner before he immigrated to America or after. Perhaps he was, as Karl had suggested, shedding "Muller" for a reason; possibly, to escape his past. But if he'd taken his wife's name upon marriage, then that was just sort of unusual. Then again, it was also his original last name. I paused: Did this mean, in some alternate universe, that I was really . . . Alex Muller?!

But back to the point: Ensch had confirmed *chi1k*'s research. A few days after her (or his) initial response, *chi1k* offered an addendum to her/his post:

> *Henry Wagner and his father in law Henry Wagner came to the USA together. There is one passenger list which agrees with this and matches up pretty well with another Wagner family from Esch-sur-Alzette.*

So Eva/Anna's father, Henry Wagner's father-in-law, was coincidentally also named . . . Henry Wagner. And my great-grandfather had traveled with this other clan of Wagners to the United States, posing as one of them—otherwise, you had to figure, he would have been listed as He(nry)(nri)(inrich) Mu(e)ller. Apparently, this was the moment when Henri Muller became Henry Wagner—not at a wedding, not in Europe. En route to America. This, in turn, suggested something possibly shady: Henry Wagner was immigrating to the United States undercover. Why else identify himself with a clan of Wagners—and enter the New World using their last name (which, to be fair, happened also to be his birth name)?

Maybe Karl's rumor about something questionable happening during the Franco-Prussian War hadn't been so off the mark. Perhaps Great-Grandfather Henry Wagner, formerly Mu(e)ller, had something he wanted to get away from in Luxembourg—and wanted to make sure it couldn't follow him across the Atlantic to America. So he found a new family.

chi1k next provided a link to a document from the ship *Algeria* of the Cunard Line, which arrived in New York on June 5, 1871.

Traveling on board was a large family by the name of Wagner:

Henri Wagner, age 50 [born about 1821]

Catherine Wagner, age 42 [born about 1829]

Eva Wagner, age 16 [born about 1855]

Eliza Wagner, age 11 [born about 1860]

Nicolas Wagner, age 8 [born about 1863]

James Wagner, age 5 [born about 1866]

Herman Wagner, age 3 [born about 1868]

and

Henri Wagner, age 22 [born about 1849]

Well, this was somewhat confusing. As far as we could tell, my great-grandfather, born Henri Wagener, had, at some point in his early twenties, decided to leave his birthplace and travel to America as "Henri Wagner" . . . in the company of someone also named Henri Wagner. Henri Wagner the Younger apparently got along well enough with the family of Henri Wagner the Elder that he followed the Wagner clan to a tiny town in northeast Iowa and married one of his daughters, Eva Wagner (also known occasionally as Anna Wagner) several years later.

There were therefore *two* Henri Wagners that settled in the same region of the state: One was my paternal great-grandfather and the other was my paternal great-great-grandfather, but the two were not related by blood. I was infinitely confused about how this had all come to pass.

So what exactly was the relationship between Henri Wagner and Henri Wagner?

I hoped that American records might clear some of this up. *chi1k* pointed me in the direction of an obituary from a local paper circa 1926, detailing the death of Henry Wagner, "the uptown grocer"—here's what I learned from it:

> *[Henry Wagner] was born July 4, 1849 at E[s]*
> *ch, Luxemberg. As a young man he followed the*
> *occupation of teamster, being so engaged during*
> *the Franco-Prussian war of 1870 and captured*
> *by the Germans on the borders of his native*
> *land. . . . In 1871, Mr. Wagner came to America*
> *and Allamakee County with his employer, also a*
> *Mr. Henry Wagner, but no relative. Business called*
> *him back to Luxemberg shortly afterwards, but*
> *he did not remain there long, joining his employer*
> *in . . . Allamakee county where the latter had*
> *purchased land and on April 4th 1877, marrying*
> *his daughter Anna. . . .*
>
> *Shortly after their marriage Mr. and Mrs.*
> *Wagner came to Lansing and have continuously*
> *resided here ever since. Both were honest God-*

*fearing people, and by industry and frugality they
succeeded in rearing a large family and establishing
a model Christian home. . . .*

The obituary confirmed everything I knew about
Henry Wagner's travel to the United States. It also conveniently explained how Henry Wagner the Younger had
gotten his start once he'd arrived here: It was all thanks to
his father-in-law and employer, Henry Wagner the Elder.
Years before he was legally a member of their family, the
Wagner clan had taken in this young stranger, Henry, as
their own, and helped him find a wife, a job, and land to
begin anew in the United States.

Together, Henry the Younger and Anna had four-
teen children and established what was by all accounts a
"model" Christian home.

So what of Cousin Karl's theory about some dark
and tortured past being my great-grandfather's escape
from Europe? It was hard to imagine him as some sort of
Franco-Prussian War criminal; Henry Wagner the American seemed like a pretty stand-up guy. Not to mention a
fairly religious one, too. The obituary summed up a de-
voted Catholic life, with room for nothing else. Certainly
no mention of Judaism.

So, yes: At first glance, my wild theories contradicted
all the evidence I'd gathered. But if you looked at this with

my now well-trained eye, it could also strangely support them. If one was indeed Jewish by heritage—given the fact that they spoke Yiddish and drank Passover wine— but did not want to be *seen* by society as Jewish . . . then perhaps devout Catholicism was a perfect cover-up. The strategy, basically, could have been: "out-Christian the Christians." By establishing a model Catholic home and having a horde of children, Henry could have fooled everyone. Lansing society may never have thought to question his Christian status.

Was there any historical precedent for this kind of trick? I called Barbara Kessel, who had written a book called *Suddenly Jewish: Jews Raised as Gentiles Discover Their Jewish Roots.* Kessel explained that it was common for Jews to hide their religion during and after World War II. In the wake of the trauma of the Nazi pogroms and death camps, Kessel said that there were certain Jewish immi-grants who gave up on their religion: It had cost them too dearly. "From here on in," she explained to me, "they decided, 'We are not Jewish or staying in touch with our Jewish family.'"

But she added that hiding one's Jewish faith just wasn't as common in the years in question—the "1880 to 1919 experience" when He(nry)(nri)(inrich) Wag(e)-ner, formerly Mu(e)ller, would have immigrated to the United States.

There were reasons other than Nazis, of course, to hide one's Jewish roots. Kessel hypothesized it might have advanced one's career and social standing to be affiliated with the church community. And, she added, there was certainly anti-Semitism: "It was not so . . . beneficial to announce your Jewish affiliation."

Then there was the pressure to conform. "There was something romantic about being American," said Kessel. "It was aspirational." Of course, being Jewish should not have precluded being American—the American identity (and American citizenship) was not based on religion, after all. At least not officially.

The obituary raised questions as much as it answered them. What happened to Henry during the Franco-Prussian War? If you don't remember what happened in the Franco-Prussian War (I sure didn't until I started reading up on it), here's what went down: In the second half of the nineteenth century, the world was in flux. European empires were trying to conquer more land for themselves. Prussia was looking to take over the German states of Bavaria, Württemberg, and Baden. The French, meanwhile, weren't keen on this Prussian power move right in their own backyard. In the middle of these two powers was Luxembourg.

It gets more complicated: In 1870, Prince Leopold of Hohenzollern-Sigmaringen, who had Prussian ties, tried to take the Spanish crown and create a Spanish-Prussian alliance. The French did not like this *at all*. Thus began the Franco-Prussian War of 1870. Tiny Luxembourg was smack-dab in the middle of any invasion route, and the war played out in the country's backyard. In the end, the Prussians triumphed over the French. This resulted in German unification, a political development that would have serious consequences eventually leading to World War I.

So how could Henry Wagner have gotten caught up in it? This line in his obit stood out to me: *As a young man he followed the occupation of teamster, being so engaged during the Franco-Prussian war of 1870 and captured by the Germans on the borders of his native land.*

If he had indeed been captured by an enemy army, why, as his obituary stated, did he return to Luxembourg "shortly after" he'd arrived in America? Who'd ever heard of going *back* to the war-torn Old World once you'd set foot in the New? It was expensive to go back and forth across the Atlantic by ship. What kind of international "business"—run from a tiny town in northeastern Iowa—would require a trip to Luxembourg in the late 1800s? What had Henry left behind?

I was developing a theory through all this travel and research: *In becoming American, something is lost.* I knew what we'd lost in Burma (and what Burma itself had lost since we'd left), but I didn't know what Henry had lost, what our family had lost, when he came to America.

I'd need to go back to the source, to Esch-sur-Alzette. I'd put my foot on the ground and stomp around, hoping to land on my elusive family story. I'd find out what we'd lost.

CHAPTER ELEVEN

The National Archives of Luxembourg are situated on a hairpin turn overlooking a high fortress over the Alzette River. I didn't have time to enjoy the views, though: I was on the hunt for evidence about Henry Wagner's departure from Luxembourg and then his return sometime in the mid-1870s—as well as clues to why he'd made this mysterious departure in the first place.

Had Henry left, like so many others, yearning for the promise of opportunity in America? Or was he chased out of the country? Maybe he'd just been lovestruck, ready to follow his eventual wife wherever she might go? And, of course, my original question: Was there any other record that might shed more light on Henry Wagner's faith?

Was he after the same thing I was after, some sense of who he was?

I spoke to an archivist expert named Mr. Nilles. He handed me a series of government records entitled "Mouvement de la Population Luxembourgeois," a (limited) collection of papers detailing population movements in and out of the country. But Nilles's old books revealed to me that a lot of people with the last name Wagner had left Esch and returned to Esch and otherwise traveled around Luxembourg in the 1880s. I hoped that one of them was Henry Wagner but had no way of knowing for sure. And I could find nothing documenting his return home.

After a day of research and jetlag, I hit a wall and returned to my hotel. There I chatted with the night clerk. He gave me a brief history of Esch-sur-Alzette, and noted the extraordinary wealth created by a boom in the iron industry in the second half of the nineteenth century. I thought, as I listened, that perhaps Great-Grandfather Henry had returned home in the hopes of making a fortune. After all, he returned sometime between 1872 and 1877—the years of the Iron Boom. The night clerk suggested I might look to see if any family land was sold during this time, in an effort to put some cash in the Wagner/Muller pockets.

This new information gave me some much-needed direction. I spent the next day looking for any evidence that might suggest our family in Esch had eventually struck it rich—or had at least tried to—during Luxembourg's Iron Boom. In the 1871 census, I could decipher that Michael Muller's listed profession was "mine worker." Now, mining was crushing, backbreaking labor that left you with time for little else: If Michael Muller was mining well into his forties, there was little likelihood that he had enough money to be a landowner. It was evident that Henry's stepfather and family had never gotten their big payday.

As I discovered this, the man who had been helping me decipher the very nearly illegible census script proclaimed loudly: "Ah, but your family was very poor!" as if to put me, the linguistically challenged Asian American, in my place.

Defiantly, I responded: "Yes, but in America, my great-grandfather was very *rich*!"

This was mostly untrue, of course. Wagner's Bar and Grocery was not exactly upscale, though the many fancy-sounding possessions it afforded the family certainly informed my father's description of Henry as a "cultured" man and a "translator."

This research was revealing, however, that while Great-Grandfather Henry had found some success in America, his family had been poor when they were in Luxembourg. My dad—long an advocate for the poor

185

and working class—always trumpeted his own humble (if storybook) Iowa beginnings. But in retelling the story of his grandfather Henry, what always struck me as odd was my father's appreciation for his grandfather's wealth and expensive furniture. Henry's crystal and silver and mahogany were a source of pride. Being a corn-eating, stickball-playing, Catholic church–attending American was very important to my dad and his conception of self, but so was the fact that his people were "dignified" Europeans from the "merchant class." People who spoke multiple languages and ate with silver and drank from crystal. Maybe this was the most natural reaction for someone who grew up with little. But I had always wondered if it wasn't somehow also hypocritical: claiming to be one thing and simultaneously fawning over its opposite.

This was in many ways the crux of the American immigrant story: the penniless arrival who made his way up the economic ladder. The rags-to-riches story is important to Americans; it's in many ways the backbone of our society, the dream we are encouraged to strive for. Even if Henry Wagner's wealth had ultimately evaporated, it was something later generations held on to (as my father had), a reminder that they were once important.

And what if that money came from someplace . . . unethical? What if the foundations of that success were built on someone else's land? What if it required the sacrifice of entire nations who remained unrecognized? My father was a well-intentioned liberal who promoted equality, but he still clung to his connection to prosperity and "high culture"—without considering that it might have been gained through questionable means.

And now that apparent hypocrisy deepened: Those classy beginnings and that imagined European education were perhaps not true, but were just stories we'd told ourselves that had little in common with reality. In fact, Henry Wagner was the "illegitimate" stepson of a miner, a man who worked as an ox-cart driver in a little mining town and smuggled himself out with a new family.

I went in search of photos from this era in the Luxembourg National Library collection, black-and-white images from the heyday of the country's mining era. Industry may have been booming, but you wouldn't know that from the look of the land and its people. The dirt roads and empty streets of downtown Esch were hardly bustling. Businesses appeared few and far between. Mining factories on the outskirts of the city were huge industrial wastelands. The miners posed outside the mouths of the mines with grim, determined faces.

Seeing these pictures made me understand the piercing poverty of the era. The darkness of soot, the meagerness of this existence. It was as far from the lace and silver and mahogany and a good Christian life as you could imagine. Those signs of wealth were perhaps just props for our American play, and if you pushed just a little bit, the scenic background gave way to reveal dust and wires and filth behind it.

I'd uncovered Henry Wagner's economic background but had yet to unravel the central family mystery of this European trip: Was he—or anyone in his immediate family—Jewish? In retelling his story, Henry Wagner had glossed over—or left out—his meager beginnings, so it didn't seem like much of a stretch to guess he could have rewritten his religious affiliation as well.

An 1867 census I came across listed Henry's mother and father as Catholic. The same went for the family Henry eventually married into, the *other* Wagner clan. All registered Catholics.

I wondered whether Henry's mother, Anne Marie, had been raised Jewish, and later converted to Christianity after her marriage to Michael Muller. After all, Judaism is passed down through the maternal line. I began looking for census records for Anne Marie's father, Pierre Wagener.

The Luxembourg government was not in the practice of asking about religion until nearly the mid-nineteenth century: If I wanted information about Pierre's faith, I'd have to search for records *after* 1867. Which wasn't going to be easy: Pierre Wagener was born in the year 1782, so he would have been age eighty-five by then. But the only Pierre Wagener of Esch-sur-Alzette listed in the 1867 census was twenty-seven years old. And thus the search for Jewish origins seemed doomed. I'd followed the increasingly poorly marked trail right into the mists of time, where everything vanished. Was my search hopeless?

I stood for a moment and wondered: What was I thinking, traveling to Luxembourg with scant knowledge of French or German, no archival research skills to speak of, and complete ignorance about genealogical detective work? I decided to retrace my steps out of this fog and go home to the familiar place I could navigate. Where the names of the people were not an endless variation of Henry, Heinrich, Henri, Anne Marie, Anna, and Anne. Where it did not seem out of the ordinary that an Asian woman might have European roots.

Home: A place full of chaos and ambition! A place with many different kinds of brown people with many different grandparents. Where I felt like I understood, and I could see myself. I could not see myself in Luxembourg City. Ever. It was, technically, my family home—but for other people, a long time ago. The national motto of Luxembourg is "We Will Remain What We Are." Well, as it concerned my family of Luxembourgers, we sure hadn't remained what we were: I could look in the mirror and know that we had become something else.

I wasn't giving up entirely, though. Once I returned home to the States, I decided to find someone who spoke the language; someone who could uncover, with certain finality, what our religious roots were, and whether there had been any reason to drop them along the way.

After many phone calls and dead ends, I came across Julie Cahill Tarr, a genealogist who spoke the language *and* had family from Luxembourg *and* was based in the Midwest. Together, she and I distilled my feelings of confusion and despair into a few distinct and (hopefully) answerable questions:

Was Henry Wagner Jewish—or was there any evidence of Judaism in his family?

Why did he leave Luxembourg, and was it, in fact, under questionable circumstances?

How did Henry, a teamster from a mining town, come to be a man of the merchant class once he arrived in America? (Where did all that fine china come from? How'd he get the cash to open Wagner's Bar and Grocery?)

Cahill Tarr went to the Luxembourg American Cultural Society and Research Center, located in Wisconsin. She combed through old copies of the *Luxemburger Gazette* and consulted colleagues who knew about German military history. She examined auction notices and passenger manifests and even more census data than I had. She even read nineteenth-century city liquor and bond permits from Allamakee County. Still, there were questions left unanswered.

To begin with, she could find no evidence that anyone in Henry Wagner's family—neither his in-laws, nor his stepfather—was Jewish or practiced Judaism. They were listed as Catholic on all available government records. This, combined with the exceedingly Christian obituary written for my great-grandfather Henry Wagner—including his funeral at the Church of the Immaculate Conception and burial at Gethsemane Cemetery—led Cahill Tarr to the conclusion that the Jewish mystery of the Wagner clan was solved.

The Wagner clan wasn't Jewish.

She proposed that my great-uncle Leo, the one who had referred to himself as "just an old Jew" all those years ago, might have converted. But this seemed unlikely. Nothing about his known biography would suggest a desire to break away from family tradition. So maybe he was just drunk on Mogen David wine. And maybe Henry Wagner learned Yiddish as one of the tools of his trade? I realized I knew close to nothing about the Jewish diaspora in Luxembourg—an admittedly very specific field of study—so I emailed Neil Jacobs, a former professor of Yiddish linguistics at Ohio State University.

The professor wrote back promptly, explaining that, first of all, Yiddish was not an obscure form of communication at the end of the nineteenth century. It was a hugely popular language: in the years preceding World War II, there were eleven to thirteen million speakers. Secondly—and more important—was I sure that Henry Wagner actually *spoke* Yiddish fluently? "When you say 'spoke,'" Professor Jacobs said, "that could mean 'really good at it for three minutes, but not three hours.'"

If Henry's command of the language was more the former (three minutes) than the latter (three hours), Jacobs added, then it was indeed possible that he'd simply picked up certain Yiddish phrases and slang as part of his trade.

My thus-far-imagined kinship with the Jewish people was indeed just a dream. The Jewish Theory had started an epic journey into my ancestry, which then introduced me to other, equally compelling mysteries. I didn't necessarily need to be Jewish to be something other than what I thought I was. There were plenty of family realities that set me apart from who I imagined the Wagners had been. Among them: mining, poverty, and possibly even criminal behavior.

With one mystery down, there were still others to solve: Were some of the Wagners chased out of Europe for treason? Was Henry Wagner a wanted man? Why did his people leave?

In my mind, this is how it went:

Henry Wagner, born into poverty in the mining town of Esch-sur-Alzette, Luxembourg, was a so-called illegitimate child who'd never known comfort. His adopted father worked several miles deep underground, swinging a pickax in the mines. The son knew nothing more of life than grime and boiled potatoes. But he had ambition. In his early teens, he began carting goods in and around town, trying to sell them for cash. This offered Henry's first glimpse into the finer things in life—the lace curtains and china and crystal goblets that decorated the homes of the wealthy, items that he would perhaps one day buy for his own family. But how? He had nothing in this meager existence. He felt like a nobody.

Then war broke out.

The Franco-Prussian War was fought on tight battle lines, and Luxembourg stood firmly at its center. Now, suddenly, Henry's hometown was bustling and chaotic, as people and things crossed its borders, headed one way or another. Supplies were needed—dry goods, ammunition, weapons—and Henry Wagner had a horse and wagon to carry them. Here, perhaps, was a business opportunity.

Suddenly, he became a young man in demand, shuttling supplies to the French on Monday, to the Prussians on Wednesday. He was playing both sides. It was miraculous how easy it was—but he knew it wouldn't last forever. By the end of 1870, there was already talk that the war would soon be ending. The Prussian army—with whom Henry had ingratiated himself, on days when he wasn't ingratiating himself with the French—was filled with commanders who noticed this young hustler, helping them one day, their enemies the next. They saw his split allegiance—and they did not like being played for fools. It was an abomination! They started asking questions.

Henry, who by now had a sizable savings squirreled away underneath his hay-filled mattress, began thinking about the next chapter, his escape from Esch, its grime and boiled potatoes. He considered other parts of Europe, but the Prussian empire was growing, and punishment could follow him across the borders. He was young, and he wasn't ready to leave the bustle and the chaos and the excitement—he had gotten a taste for this life. He wanted something different, something where his future could be shaped anew. He'd heard stories about America. But how to get there? He knew no one in the United States, didn't even speak the language. He would need people, resources.

Another man on the teamster circuit, older and slower but still strong, mentioned that he intended to leave soon. He'd had enough of this place, he said. He'd heard of the American land, too, and he wanted a piece of it. It was too fortunate, as if God himself had laid out the plan: This other man happened to have the same name as Henry's mother's family! It would be easy to change the papers and make it look as if they were one family. Could they leave soon? Yes, said the elder Wagner, they would leave soon. Better to get out now, while everyone is still distracted by war. (*Better to get out now*, thought Henry, *before anyone finds out what I did*.)

So went my fantasy about Henry's story.

That is not quite what happened.

Cahill Tarr explained to me that the records about Franco-Prussian prisoners of war were not exactly in tip-top shape. If Henry had been captured by the Germans and/or accused of treasonous behavior during the war, there were few records to prove it.

But she did stumble upon information that at least pointed in the *direction* of questionable activities that might have driven Henry, his future father-in-law Henry Wagner the Elder, and his family out of Europe and over to America. For one, they'd exited Europe via England or Ireland, rather than leaving for America directly from Luxembourg, as was custom—perhaps to evade whoever might be interested in their whereabouts. And there were signs that they had left in a hurry, as if they were fleeing: they'd put their house up for auction as a way to sell it as quickly as possible.

While this information didn't offer any certainty, it

did present an answer to a question I'd been wondering all along: Where did Henry Wagner the Younger get that money to start his own business, Wagner's Bar and Grocery, in Lansing, Iowa? Henry Wagner the Elder's home sale offered one clue.

This future father-in-law's home was listed as a three-story house with a slated roof, a cellar, and a stable for twelve (!) horses. The house was located near the local church, which suggested it was in a good neighborhood. And it came with a separate garden plot, also for sale.

Julie Cahill Tarr came to this conclusion: "The proceeds from the [home] sale were probably more than enough for the family's passage to America and may have been enough for them to get a head start settling in Iowa."

But all of this raised a question: How did Henry Wagner the Elder, carter of random goods, make the cash to buy a home like his in the first place? Perhaps, then, Henry the Elder had been engaged in what I loosely categorized as a side hustle, aka *a little of this and a little of that*. And maybe some of this (or that) involved selling on the black market or, later, hauling goods for both the French and the Germans during wartime. Equally involved in this side hustle might have been his employees—and who was working for him at the time but my great-grandfather: Henry Wagner.

What I hadn't understood until this point was precisely

how close Henry Wagner the Younger had been to Henry Wagner the Elder (no relation). Cahill Tarr revealed that the younger man had been in the employ of the older as far back as the Old World. Therefore, if one of them was engaged in a criminal side hustle, so might the other have been—giving both a reason to flee Esch as soon as the going got tough. But would they really have tied their fortunes so closely together? After all, it was one thing to work for a guy; it was another thing to start a whole new life with him (and his family) in America.

As it turns out, the bonds between the two men were even deeper than I'd thought.

Cahill Tarr had determined that, according to the 1867 Luxembourg census, Henry Wagner *lived in the same house* as Henry Wagner the Elder—his eventual father-in-law. On both of their (separate) census entries, the same address was listed—a fact that slipped by my reading of the same document. This meant that for a time, Henry Wagner had lived quite comfortably—or at least not in a hovel with only grime and potatoes. In fact, Henry had been inside one of those well-furnished homes himself, drinking from actual glasses, sleeping on a mattress and not a cot. Perhaps this is where he got his taste for the finer things in life—and perhaps this is what drove him to do whatever he had to do to get out of Esch. Once he'd lived amid wealth, he wanted more of it for himself.

The knowledge that the two Wagner men, Elder and Younger, had once shared the same roof was, in effect, the key to the biggest mystery of them all: Why had my great-grandfather ended up hitching his wagon to that of a random family, forever linking his fate and fortune with theirs? It also explained how he met my eventual great-grandmother, Eva/Anna Wagner. They'd shared the same home address!

This clarified a lot. Nearly all of the big, looming questions, in fact. But there were all kinds of subtler questions I'd never know the answer to, including: Why? Why did they live together? Did something happen to the Muller family, or the Wagner family? Was Michael Muller a friend of Henry Wagner the Elder's? Had my great-grandfather always had his eye on Eva/Anna, the woman who would become his eventual wife in America? Was theirs a romance for the ages, or did Henry just marry her because it would secure his share of that Wagner money?

I'd mistakenly believed that all this sleuthing would give me a key with which I could paint by numbers to get a full-color image of our family and its characters. What I got instead were fragments—and things I would never truly know. Too many of the papers had been lost, or maybe never existed in the first place. The things that would have been most illuminating in the search, the conversations between people, were long forgotten. I would have to fill in the blanks and decide for myself what I believed. Just as in Mandalay, I would have to determine my end point; there was no finish line.

Still, I had enough information about what we'd done and how we'd lived, the choices we'd made along the way, to conclude that we were not who I'd been told we were: models of virtue, defenders of the faith, as American as apple pie. We lied and cheated occasionally and did our best to survive. We told one another stories that made us seem somehow of better character than other arrivals in our United States. And so this was what it meant to be an American, as far as my family was concerned: a fairy tale about perseverance, loyalty, and faith. We tried to forget the rest. But the rest was a foundational part of who we were, and what our true community was.

I may not have been Jewish, but I could already see a new kind of identity forming. From these trips to Esch and Rangoon, I understood that my people were in some cases flawed. They skimmed over their own histories. My mother's family held the past closer—the Old World was very much still with her in custom, language, and cuisine—while my father's side had become more generically American. But both sides had crafted an identity that buried the uncomfortable truths of the past: my great-grandfather U Myint Kaung played a role in Burma's economic disasters; my grandmother Mya Mya

Gyi harbored racist sentiments that formed the dark side of Burmese nationalism. Henry Wagner buried the truth in Esch-sur-Alzette—his struggle, his possible crimes, the debts he owed to others.

Even the land on which we'd grown food had once belonged to someone else. The soil wasn't really ours; its fruits were the rightful property of the tribes that had preceded us. The success we'd had in later years had been lopsided: We'd won because others had been forced to lose. We'd flourished in a country that excluded black and brown people from the very same possibilities. What sort of honor was there in that?

I was not Jewish, I didn't feel particularly Burmese, and Luxembourg might as well have been Pluto. But in all these places, all these cities, I saw glimpses of who my real people might have been. Carved from the negative space of my family history, I saw who we actually were. We were storytellers, revisionists, and sometimes even liars. We built our future selves on deceit and half-truths, we plastered our cracks with omissions—as well as genuine courage and smarts and will. In this act of re-creation, we became Americans. And I guess there was some kind of belonging in that.

PART IV

THE CROSSHAIRS

CHAPTER TWELVE

I belonged in the crosshairs, the areas in-between. This realization hit me when I found myself at the National Archives in London, doing further research on my Burmese family history. The Rangoon archives had proved so fruitless that I'd gone to see what Britain had preserved of their time in Burma. Maybe there would be journals or photos that could shed light on my great-grandmother Daw Thet Kywe's era, the heyday of British rule.

Inside the archives, I found yellowing manuscripts, accounts of imperial Burma from the mid-1800s, written with various levels of curiosity, disgust, racism, and distinctly British humor. Many were compiled by British officers stationed in the country.

Of the information I could gather, the most compelling

person I learned about was Mindon Min, the last great king of Burma, the second-to-last ruler of the Konbaung dynasty, who reigned from 1853 until his death in 1878. Among other things, Mindon Min created the world's largest book, a canon of Theravada Buddhist teachings known as the *Tipitaka,* and published a newspaper, the *Mandalay Gazette.* He—perhaps more importantly—believed in freedom of speech.

Mindon Min, according to these texts, was a shrewd leader who never accepted the word of his courtiers as truth. He had spies everywhere. According to historians, they included "monks, queens, princes, princesses, ladies-in-waiting, senior and junior officials, members of the *ahmudan* class [crown service groups], holy men, nuns, medicine men, masseurs and barbers."

Among the cohort of men and women who made it their duty to attend to the whims of Mindon Min and his four wives was my grandmother's grandmother, an attendant to the court. In our family, this fact was always relayed with pride, but as I discovered in a listing of the various personages . . . there were a lot of attendants at Mindon Min's court.[1]

Personal Attendants in the Court

35 pages who carried the royal insignia on
state occasions

40 royal tea servers
  60 bearers of the royal betel box and other
     personal utensils
 100 royal slipper bearers
  40 bearers of the royal white umbrellas
  10 lectors, who read aloud from religious
     books
  15 grooms of the chamber, who acted as
     messengers
 450 gentlemen-at-arms
 220 bearers of the royal swords in state
     processions
 155 chamberlains or lictors, a company of men
     chosen for their height and whose duties
     also included the policing of the palace

That was a lot of royal slippers. As the British de-tailed it, Burmese court life was almost absurdly rules-based; shoes, for example, were never to be worn in the presence of the king.[2] But an accounting of these courtly flourishes tended to distract from the most important part of Mindon Min's rule: he shepherded Burma through the last, truly golden days of a semi-independent, pre-British state. It sounded like my great-great-grandmother had worked for a fairly decent boss, insofar as the king was her boss.

I was fascinated to read about the last years of independent Burma. In 1852, after the southern half of Burma fell to the Brits, Queen Victoria plotted to expand her dominion north. Mindon Min, seeing British imperial power closing over his kingdom, reached out for the hand of the French, the mortal enemy of the British. The hope was that a Burmese-French partnership would protect Burma from a British invasion.

By 1873, Mindon Min's corps of diplomats signed a treaty with France.[3] Around the same time, the French were coming off a war over several German states. The country was aggressively ambitious during this particular period—remember that French concern over German unification under the Prussians eventually led to the Franco-Prussian War. And just three years earlier, the same two powers had been fighting over control of Luxembourg.

As the English saw things, it was time to contain the French. They observed France's aggression in Europe, coupled with the country's recent advances in Indochina (now Cambodia, Laos, and Vietnam), and they didn't like it. Nor did they appreciate Mindon Min's new trade partnership with France.

Meanwhile, in Burma, Mindon Min was aging. Sensing his looming death, his son Thibaw orchestrated the murder of any and all royal children who might pose a threat to his own rise to the throne. Fratricide and patricide were not uncommon measures to secure the crown (in Burma and elsewhere*) but the scale of the slaughter made it one for the Burmese history books. Upon learning of it, the British were both horrified and skeptical, although crown carnage was not exactly an alien concept to them.

British-Burmese relations under Mindon Min, while largely peaceable, had frayed, especially with the French in the picture. Where did the new king Thibaw's sympathies lie? Thibaw, increasingly in debt, took a page from what was now a fairly well-worn playbook: he reached out to the French.

The British had grown tired of Burmese efforts to pit one imperial superpower against another. They issued a strict ultimatum demanding that the king relinquish his rule and hand over Upper Burma . . . or else.[4] Perhaps unsurprisingly, Thibaw—a king who had overseen the slaughter of the entire royal family in order to take the throne—refused.

With Burma woefully overpowered and outgunned, the Third Anglo-Burmese War did not last long. The end of the Konbaung dynasty—a dynasty that had spanned 133 years—was brought about in precisely thirteen days. On November 27, 1886, the British seized all of Burma,

---

* Too many countries in Europe to count, plus lots of Asia and the Mideast (and Africa, Latin America, and Oceania, undoubtedly).

raising their own flag over Mandalay, where it would hang for over half a century.

Thibaw and his queen Supayalat had been sent off to India, the other country ruled under the British Raj. The Burmese royal court was no longer, and the men and women who once acted as messengers, astrologists, and advisers were killed or cast off to live as common folk in the capital city of Mandalay, outside the palace gates.

Among those who survived this wildly tumultuous period of Burmese court life was my great-great-grandmother, Daw Thet Kywe's mother. We don't know exactly when she left the court—whether she stayed on until the end of Thibaw's reign or left after Mindon Min died. We just know that somehow—as part of the spoils—she bought that teak house across the street from St. Francis Xavier Church and around the corner from the Wesleyan Methodist mission school. The house I'd seen in photos, and maybe the house I'd found a few months prior as I was stumbling around Mandalay on a wild-goose chase for memories.

I'd long assumed that nothing, other than *me,* connected Rangoon and Esch-sur-Alzette. After all, if you stretched a wire from one city to the other, it would span more than half the globe. Ninety years separated Henry Wagner's decision to leave the Old World and Mya Mya Gyi's to become a Westerner.

But what dawned on me at this moment, sitting in the climate-controlled stacks of the British Library reading a dusty old history book, was the intersection of my two family histories. If there had never been a bloody European land skirmish in the nineteenth century, there might not have been a Franco-Prussian War. If Henry Wagner and his future father-in-law had never gotten tangled up in the Franco-Prussian War, they might not have left for America.

In the same way, if there never had been a bloody European land skirmish in the nineteenth century, the British might well have left Upper Burma alone.

The Burmese court might have stayed intact and the British would never have gained full control of the country.

The military junta that seized power in a coup and subsequently drove my grandmother and mother off to the United States . . . might never have come to power.

I now understood that there was indeed a connection between Burma and Luxembourg that had nothing to do with me: both countries had been bystanders in the same feud of nations, tested for loyalty, and exchanged as a show of power. Daw Thet Kywe and Henry Wagner (the Younger) had more in common than I'd realized.

The Europeans—and their territorial aggressions— had upended two people on opposite sides of the globe, for very different reasons, at the very same time. I was but one small outcome of all of this, but the mingling of fate and fortune had started decades, centuries earlier. America was the beginning, a new chapter—but in a weird way, it was also the conclusion of a story that had begun a long time ago.

CHAPTER THIRTEEN

In all my research and reading and traveling, there was something I hadn't yet tried: examining my DNA it-self. The information I'd been uncovering all this time had given me a firmer grasp on my family history, but parts of it still remained abstract. I'd set foot in the cities where our lost lives lingered like ghosts. I'd hoped to find peace or a sense of belonging, some lifeline to my heri-tage. Instead, I had found a complicated, confusing (more truthful) understanding of who I was, of my people.

But there was another way to investigate the past, a universal language that could pinpoint me—and only me. It was my genetic makeup, the evidence of exactly where I'd come from. DNA could reveal precisely who my peo-ple were—and whether there were chapters in our story that my family members had glossed over or deleted. Beyond that, science would tell me exactly how many cultures my identity truly spanned. The movements of empires, the costs of war, the ambitions of peoples would be mirrored in my blood. I'd know where I came from and to whom I belonged—and in a technically precise way. No more reliance on chat rooms or archivists or dusty books. The information was within me!

What would science have to say?

Thanks to technology, there were multiple DNA test services that offered incredible promises in their online advertisements for this kind of self-questioning. At this point, there were several options for DNA-based ancestry tests—three of the most popular were Family Tree DNA, 23andMe, and AncestryDNA. I didn't know which might return the most comprehensive information and therefore decided to do several of them. I figured I'd combine the results and determine at least the general coordinates of my heritage, if not the pinpointed locations.*

On my mother's side, I wondered how closely the results would correspond with what I'd determined over the past several months about my Asian heritage. It was possible that the DNA wouldn't show me anything new, but who knew? My mother and grandmother were not

---

* All the information that follows about the genetic-ancestry industry is true as of the time of writing; the specific science and practices are, of course, in a state of constant flux.

214

just Burmese—they were unquestioningly Burmese, in the same way that someone is allergic to cashews or is left-handed. As far as they knew, we had never lived anywhere else, never been anyone else. My father had a story about his heritage, but it was never airtight: He had grown up knowing that we came from Europe, and this offered an opening for an origin story that *might* be different from what he'd imagined. No such possibility existed in my maternal line. The people who had come to America were still alive, and they could attest to the fact that there was no mystery surrounding our roots, about who we'd been before arrival on these shores. And their answer was this: they were Burmese. They had never bothered to consider anything else, mostly because there was no need to.

As for my father's side of the family, I had essentially given up on the Jewish Theory at this point, though some tiny part of me still hoped my DNA would offer a rebuttal to all the evidence I'd gathered so far and reveal that I had Ashkenazi blood. But mostly I wanted to see if—mixed with the Irish and Luxembourgian blood—there might be something unique or surprising hidden away.

This is what DNA testing offers people: mystery, strangeness, specialness. The suggestion that maybe you descended from the pharaohs, that your particular blackness wasn't born of slavery but of untouched African blood—as if your people miraculously escaped the horrors and the violence, the exiles and escapes, the flights and trauma, and existed as exceptions to the American rule. Perhaps your Mexican roots are royal Mayan, or your red hair comes from the Vikings, not the Scots.

Part of me wondered about all this. Was DNA testing a way to search for evidence that we were each made of special stock? If I was being truthful, that's exactly what I still wanted to have confirmed. The more I knew about my family, the more information I had about their compromises and crimes, their weaknesses and failures . . . the more intense my yearning became to find something extraordinary, something mythic buried beneath these newly unearthed facts. As if to balance out the mundane, messy reality of this family history. I wanted something epic. Don't we all?

The Family Tree DNA test boasted the "most comprehensive Y chromosome, autosomal, and mitochondrial ancestry DNA database for genetic genealogists." Their website assured me that it would trace ancestral lines with scientific rigor.

If Family Tree DNA positioned itself as the most clinically comprehensive of the top tests, the service offered by a company called 23andMe* was the most

---

* 23andMe, if you were wondering, is a reference to the twenty-three pairs of chromosomes that most humans are born with—and that carry the DNA within which the genetic code is written.

user-friendly—and seemingly the most high-tech. The company began operations in 2006 with the goal of providing specific, personalized DNA-based information. Customers could investigate their own genes, and discover whether diseases or cancers ran in their bloodlines. The point of sharing this data, 23andMe said, was to increase people's awareness about their health and the illnesses carried in their families.

Critics of this practice made the point that society should also consider how factors unrelated to genetics—such as environment, economic stability, and access to health care—could inform someone's health outcomes as much as his or her genealogy. And that, not insignificantly, you would have to be careful when giving people potentially devastating information: Were they prepared for it? Was society prepared for it? What happened if you started marginalizing entire communities based on their DNA-based tendency toward something terrible? Health data could be heavy stuff, if handled improperly.

But wasn't it better to have people aware of various hideous illnesses than . . . to leave them unaware of various hideous illnesses? Genetic scientists made the argument that their conclusions wouldn't necessarily condemn entire subsets of American society, and actually that their goal was to do the very opposite. Give people the information, get them the help and medicine they needed. Information was power! Or so they claimed.

The FDA disagreed. According to the government, people could misread their health data with disastrous consequences. Without proper care and information, they might try to self-medicate, get unnecessary surgeries, or disregard drug therapies—all outcomes that could endanger an individual's health. The FDA asserted that the science was faulty and hadn't received the necessary approvals. Plus, they said, these companies were compiling individuals' results into databases that were then sold to other companies, which appeared to be unethical—this was private information, after all!

In the wake of the FDA's decision in 2013 to put a halt to the company's health testing, 23andMe pivoted to the business of DNA-based ancestry reports. Apparently, in the eyes of the regulators, information about possible Croatian ancestry was less explosive than being told you were a carrier of a rare disease. This became a strategy to stay in the business of DNA without worrying that inaccuracy might somehow lead to health issues. And it worked. By late 2015, the company had more than a million users, double what it had at the time of the FDA's ruling.[1]

If 23andMe had come to ancestry services in round-about fashion, the even more unlikely story was that of

AncestryDNA, a genealogical search service run by industry heavyweight Ancestry, a for-profit company whose founders were members of the Church of Jesus Christ of Latter-day Saints. Admittedly, it was easier for me to skip lightly over the involvement of faith, given my own confused religious upbringing.

So I decided to do all three tests: Family Tree DNA, 23andMe, *and* AncestryDNA. There was no harm in overnighting as much saliva and cheek-swabbed cellular DNA as possible to as many processing centers that would take it. What could go wrong?

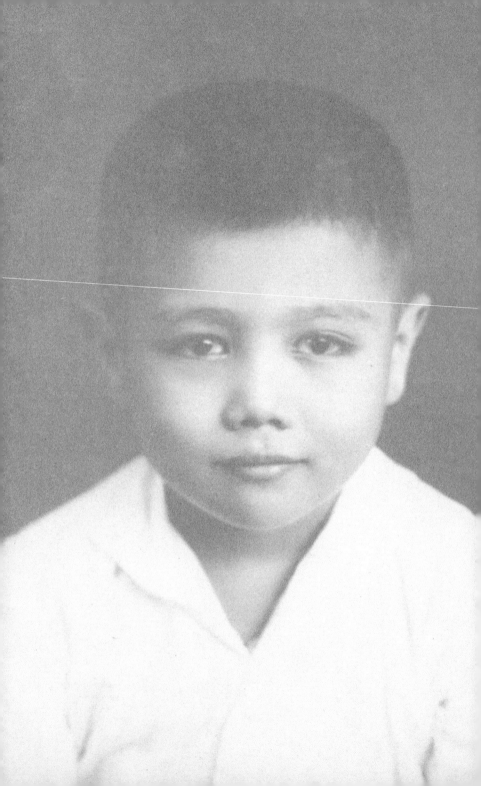

CHAPTER FOURTEEN

I was certainly afflicted with the narcissism of self-testing, eager for data about *me me me* that would separate me from the rest of the world. Was it too harsh to say that DNA-based ancestry testing was a selfish exercise? Sure, *some* people were taking the test to see how interconnected we were as a species—to get scientific confirmation of the hidden bonds that linked us to one another. But I couldn't help wondering if the makers of these tests were profiting off precisely the opposite: the quest to turn *inward* rather than *outward,* to look for differences between us rather than similarities. To help us each find the thing that makes us unique, as if we could somehow free ourselves from the rest of humanity's stresses and demands.

This had long been a philosophical quest; now we had technology to aid our search.

This kind of personal validation did not come cheaply. All the tests I purchased cost between one hundred and three hundred dollars per kit! If you limited your testing to one person and one test, you might be able to call it a deal. But once you were hooked on the addictive practice of ancestry testing, chances were that you'd probably want to get your mother and father involved—just, you know, to *get a little more information.* And if that information was weird or juicy or in some way controversial, you'd probably buy a few more tests for your uncle in Chiang Mai, Thailand, or your cousin in La Crosse, Wisconsin.

People were giving the DNA kits out as Christmas presents, birthday presents, anniversary gifts. It seemed odd (to me, at least) that Santa Claus would leave the truth about one's ancestral heritage under the Christmas tree, but the more I talked to friends and family about what I was doing, the keener their interest became. By the end of this project, I'd easily spent well over two thousand dollars on an array of DNA-based ancestry kits, most for this project, some handed out as gifts. Despite the popularity of these tests, most people taking them were entirely in the dark about the technology they used. They took the test and waited, hoping for news that would scientifically affirm—or transform—who they were and where they came from.

Each service's website includes lots of convincing science talk—you can't help feeling like you're in very professional hands. Some of the kits rely on spit samples, saliva that's collected using a small vial with a spit guard. Other tests use the DNA from a cheek swab, which is taken via a doll-sized toothbrush. Both devices are unlike anything you might ever normally come across.

I started out by testing myself. After all, my DNA would have genetic information about both Henry Wagner and U Myint Kaung, whereas my parents' would show only their own European or Asian bloodlines. Still, it would be necessary to test them, too. To obtain the fullest picture of our family lineage, I wanted the biggest data set. The more people tested, the clearer the picture. And the older they are, the farther back the genetic information.

Over the course of two afternoons, I swabbed my cheeks with the Thumbelina-sized toothbrush for the Family Tree DNA. This was not as easy as it would seem, mostly because you must wait one hour after you eat or drink anything, and I am apparently a very thirsty and hungry person who consumes something liquid or solid approximately every forty-seven minutes. In the end, I had to set a timer to remind myself not to put food or drink in my mouth.

Once that was complete, I dropped the swabbed toothbrush head into a small vial of preserving liquid, registered my kit online, packed the sample in a padded envelope, and sent it off to be analyzed in what I could only imagine was a gleaming lab populated by white-coated genius geneticists.

A few words about enlisting my parents in the project: It had been some time since I asked them for a favor. Even as a child, I'd never asked for much, and as far as I can recall, they weren't particularly hands-on as it concerned my upbringing. My mother bragged that she had never had to wake me up for class or bother me about schoolwork, and my father was often at work, a phantom who came home late. They roused themselves briefly to object to my choice of college but then lapsed back into whatever the opposite of helicopter parenting is.

I was on my own when it came to my professional life—only after I'd accepted a job offer did my parents find out I was even interested in a field of journalism. ("You're covering the White House now?" they'd say, in delighted surprise. "You're going to be hosting a TV show? That's great!" as if I were telling them that I had planned a vacation to Belize.)

In fact, the requests I made those days tended toward

asking them to take better care of *themselves*—to go see the cardiologist (my mother) or the physician (my father)—or the occasional fact-check on a detail as it concerned the family recipe for chicken with tangerine peels (Mom) or the 1972 Iowa caucus (Dad). Inviting them to take part in something like a DNA test made me slightly nervous—and I hoped they would agree to it.

My mother was, characteristically, slightly baffled by the whole process—she typically avoided anything concerning the internet or unfamiliar scientific processes. But she was game. She approached my grandmother about donating some of her saliva for a 23andMe test, too. My grandmother was nothing if not extremely interested in herself and so dutifully sat on the couch to take her DNA sample.

As for my father, I think he was somewhat skeptical about why he was being asked to do this. He'd given me a thorough catalog of his childhood memories and knew that I'd spoken to his sisters and my cousins to fill in the missing pieces. He knew I'd gone as far as his grandfather's birthplace of Esch-sur-Alzette. I worried that he knew I might be searching for more information on the Jewish Theory that he kept trying to put to rest rather than simply chronicling our extraordinary story of triumph and faith, as I claimed.

"I'm so interested in what we'll find!" he emailed me,

unconvincingly, upon receipt of the zippy multicolored 23andMe test kit. "When will we get results?"

I surreptitiously registered my email address for his results, in case the tests came back showing him to be indeed 24.7 percent Ashkenazi Jewish . . . or something otherwise significantly unexpected. As open-minded as I knew my father to be in his political leanings, the narrative about where he'd come from—and the ethnic traditions he'd inherited—were central to his sense of self, and he was increasingly reliant on this narrative as he got older. He felt a connection with the Irish Catholics in Washington—especially ones from the Midwest—a union that was social and cultural as much as it was professional. He had regular beers and burgers with these people; he shook their hands on Sunday after Mass before launching into political discussions. To cancel his membership in this group by proving him to *not* be Catholic might be a trauma in its own right. If the tests determined an ethnicity that shattered his expectations, I figured I'd need to walk him through the results . . . and then spend some time battling it out with him to convince him they were accurate.

I felt a healthy amount of concern about all that was at stake, but I decided to ignore it (it was far too late now, and anyway, the tests had been purchased!) and went forward, hoping for the best.

Ever since the start of this harebrained odyssey, I had been looking for community. With scientific precision, perhaps DNA could help me find my place in a sprawling, continuing narrative; confirm my role in this cast of characters; and declare, finally, that I belonged somewhere. It might reveal that I had people in Indonesia, Iran, or Tibet; or maybe "home" was just Burma and Luxembourg and always had been. No matter the result, I would find myself in a long, unbreakable chain of people. I longed to finally receive that message, beamed across time and space: You Are Not Alone.

CHAPTER FIFTEEN

Several weeks after taking the tests, the results started coming in. "Learn more about you!" the email in my in-box encouraged, and, oh, did I want to learn more about me! But first there was my mother and her results.

23andMe found she was:

55.2 percent Southeast Asian

14.9 percent Chinese

11.3 percent Broadly South Asian

8.8 percent Broadly East Asian

5.4 percent Mongolian

3.4 percent Broadly East Asian and Native American

1 percent Unassigned

less than .1 percent European

My grandmother, according to 23andMe, was:

46.9 percent Southeast Asian

13.3 percent Chinese

10.8 percent Mongolian

10.2 percent Broadly East Asian

8.8 percent Broadly South Asian

5.8 percent Broadly East Asian and Native
American

2.9 percent Unassigned (!)

1.2 percent Korean

.1 percent European

and less than .1 percent Sub-Saharan African

Both had a very hefty amount of unexpected Asian DNA: a large percentage of Chinese and Mongolian DNA. Here was an interesting turn of events.

When I asked what she thought of the DNA report, my mother said she was intrigued by the Mongolian blood. She found it "romantic," and by this I could only imagine that Genghis Khan on horseback riding across a windswept plain conjured some kind of "romance" in my mother's mind. She was thrilled with the (less than)

.1 percent European DNA result, in part because of its cosmopolitan connotations, but mostly because she had long held a fixation with Italian culture, and here was proof (however slim) that perhaps this obsession was genetic destiny.

I understood the results differently. The European DNA, originating from a nation nearly on the other side of the globe, suggested Burma's unusual and forgotten history—a time when European merchants could be found in the markets of Ava and Amarapura alike. This random strand of DNA pointed to something bigger: Burma's place on trade routes, and the cultural mixing that resulted from them.

I was energized by this result, but I was also . . . a little forlorn, self-diagnosed with a mild case of historical FOMO: Why couldn't I have been there to experience any of this? What had it been like? And why did I have to be the one who grew up in the internet era and the rise of a ruling military junta? I imagined the interactions on the streets of Amarapura, the exchanges in Italian and Burmese.

I thought of the first Mongols entering Burma, or the early Chinese comingling with the Burmans, mixing to the degree that one day they became each other, with only a border to separate them. What a rich history there was in our veins—all that past and all those peoples from centuries ago. It was in direct opposition to Luxembourg's stuffy and self-righteous motto: We Will Remain What We Are. With each successive generation, we were becoming something radically, perhaps even unrecognizably, different.

Then there was the "unassigned" DNA. What, exactly, was that? On the 23andMe website, the company offered its version of a disclaimer, freeing them of certain responsibilities:

This report can tell you:
- The location and amount of your DNA that is similar to DNA from other people with known ancestry.
- How your ancestry was likely inherited from your biological parents (if at least one of them is linked to your profile).

This report cannot tell you:
- The precise origins of all of your ancestors. The results presented here are estimates, which may change over time as our algorithm improves.
- Ancestry estimates for populations for which we do not have sufficient data.

Those were useful warnings, even if they were unclear—".1 percent European" seemed like a pretty exact "estimate," after all. What was the possibility of error? And what "populations" did the company not have data on? (What did they mean by "populations," anyway?) With doubt slowly creeping in, I began to wonder how the tests compared to one another.

I looked at my father's results to see what science had to say about him.

23andMe found he was:

48.2 percent British and Irish
25 percent French and German
18.2 percent Broadly Northwestern European
4.0 percent Broadly Southern European
1.6 percent Scandinavian
1.2 percent Broadly European
1.1 percent Italian
.7 percent Balkan

That was 100 percent European.

There was nothing in there about Eastern European blood that might suggest Ashkenazi Jewish or Sephardic Jewish DNA, or any Jewish DNA whatsoever. There was nothing left to hang the Jewish Theory on, save Henry

Wagner's reported taste for Mogen David wine—and that seemed more than shaky; it seemed desperate. To a large degree, I'd made my peace with this result, but still it stung like a lost splinter, too deep to remove.

If I was being honest, my father's test was mostly a nothingburger. There was so much "Broadly This" and "Broadly That" in the results, it made me wonder how accurately the lab technicians at 23andMe were truly able to pinpoint the DNA that made my father who he was. Convinced that spending more money on more ancestry tests would lead me to the most interesting conclusions, I asked my father to take two more tests: Family Tree DNA's Family Finder and AncestryDNA's test.

"Dad," I said, "that first test found you to be one point six percent Scandinavian! Can you imagine?" I chuckled haltingly. "Why don't you take some other tests, just so we can see what other absurd results we get back!"

Secretly, I was praying that AncestryDNA and/or Family Tree DNA would return something interesting or at least unexpected in his DNA and render all this money well spent. My father sighed and agreed to humor me. He swabbed his cheek and spit some more, then dutifully left the samples to be collected by the mailman.

When I finally got the email alert that the results were ready, AncestryDNA assessed him to be:

43 percent Western European
29 percent Irish
13 percent British
 6 percent Scandinavian
 6 percent Italian/Greek
 3 percent from the Iberian Peninsula

Again, there was no evidence of any Jewish or Eastern European DNA.

I was disappointed. My father's genetic narrative was fairly straightforward, even somewhat predictable. I realize now that I had wanted his test results to reflect the discoveries I'd made through all my research work. I wanted scientific evidence that we were more complicated, more unusual, more crooked, than my family mythology suggested. But I didn't have it.

I remembered my first lessons as a genetic detective: look for the cracks, pull on the snags, follow the leads. I began to look for quirks that might suggest error and therefore give me something worthwhile to pursue. The mysterious Scandinavian DNA was what popped out at me—and this test found even more of it. I flagged it for later; I'd get to the root of the matter, once I determined what exactly the matter was.

The last hope for science to redeem my increasingly

harebrained idea was my father's Family Tree DNA's results:

> 98 percent European (!)
> 2 percent "trace" DNA

That broke down to:

> 50 percent Western and Central Europe
> 35 percent British
> 10 percent Scandinavian
> 3 percent Southeastern European

As far as that "trace" DNA went? Family Tree specified that it was likely from Finland . . . although it might just be, as the website stated, "background noise." I stopped first to consider the fact that my father was apparently 10 percent *Scandinavian*. This was considerably more Scandi blood than either of the other tests had shown—so much more, in fact, that it was clear someone had to be wrong. And then there was the 3 percent Southeastern European blood—might this suggest Jewish blood after all? Maybe this was the test I'd been waiting for.

Family Tree DNA offered *another,* super-specific test of the male Y chromosome line that would return the ancestral origins of my father's paternal line. I decided to call their offices to get some help understanding the very clinical results. They could offer no clarity on all that Scandinavian blood. Despite the percentage of Eastern European DNA in the earlier test, no Jewish DNA matches were returned (something this test could actually scan for with some precision). Unequivocally, it seemed, Carl Wagner had no Jewish DNA on his father's side. The genetic profile of my paternal line spoke nothing of a complicated or confused narrative. We were what we had always said we were: white, Christian Europeans.

What did the collective lab results have to say about my own saliva and cheek cells? To be fair, I had probably been most interested in what the test results said about my mother's and father's genetics—their DNA went back further in time and could therefore (potentially) unearth more interesting discoveries. And yet maybe, just maybe, something dramatic would be revealed in my own results. Perhaps some bloodline that had escaped detection in previous generations—that would be the genetic triumph I'd been searching for.

When it came to me, ol' futureface, 23andMe told me I was:

37.5 percent Southeast Asian
22.1 percent French and German

21.2 percent British and Irish

5.7 percent Broadly Northwestern European

5.4 percent Broadly South Asian

4.7 percent Chinese

1.3 percent Broadly East Asian and Native American

.9 percent Broadly Southern European

.4 percent Broadly East Asian

.5 percent Unassigned (!)

.3 percent Broadly European

.1 percent Balkan

and less than .1 percent Central and South African

While AncestryDNA determined that I was:

29 percent East Asian

14 percent Scandinavian

13 percent British

10 percent Central Asian

9 percent South Asian

8 percent Irish

5 percent Polynesian

4 percent Western European

3 percent Italian/Greek

2 percent from the Iberian Peninsula

1 percent Melanesian

Plus a few traces of North African, Eastern
European, and Northwest Russian/Finnish

And Family Tree DNA's Family Finder test estimated
that I was:

32 percent Southeast Asian

13 percent British

11 percent South Central Asian

10 percent Scandinavian

8 percent Iberia

8 percent West and Central Europe

7 percent Southeast Europe

4 percent Finland

3 percent Northeast Asia

2 percent Siberia

Plus more "trace" percentages from Oceania
and East Europe

Unlike my mother and grandmother, I showed no
specific Mongolian DNA. One test showed me to have a
hefty dose of Irish (8 percent), while another found that
I had nearly the same amount of DNA from the Iberian

Peninsula. One test said I was 5 percent Polynesian, but the other two found no Polynesian. Beyond the broad breakdown of "Asian" DNA to "European" DNA, it was a toss-up. There were wild variations in these smaller percentages and completely different assessments as to what my genetic makeup was.

And then there was the mysterious "unassigned" or "trace" category, which appeared on my DNA results, as well as my mother's and grandmother's. This DNA was *unlike most of what they'd observed before,* like a rare plant or three-winged bird. It was also referred to as *background noise,* which sounded suspicious.

The inconsistencies and unknowns rang a few alarm bells. Clearly something was off if I was being told I was nearly a tenth Irish and a twentieth Polynesian and maybe a little bit Native American and also . . . none of these things at all.

Which brings me to the lingering Scandinavian question: AncestryDNA asserted I was 14 percent Scandinavian, while Family Tree DNA determined that I was 10 percent Scandinavian and 4 percent Finnish. But this was also, weirdly, nearly as much Northern European DNA as my father had, if not slightly more—which seemed questionable at best, given the fact that my mother had approximately 0 percent Scandinavian or Finnish blood. And then there was 23andMe, which concluded I had no Scandinavian or Finnish DNA whatsoever. What was going on here?

Surely I was not the first person in history to receive an ancestry report and find the results less than convincing.

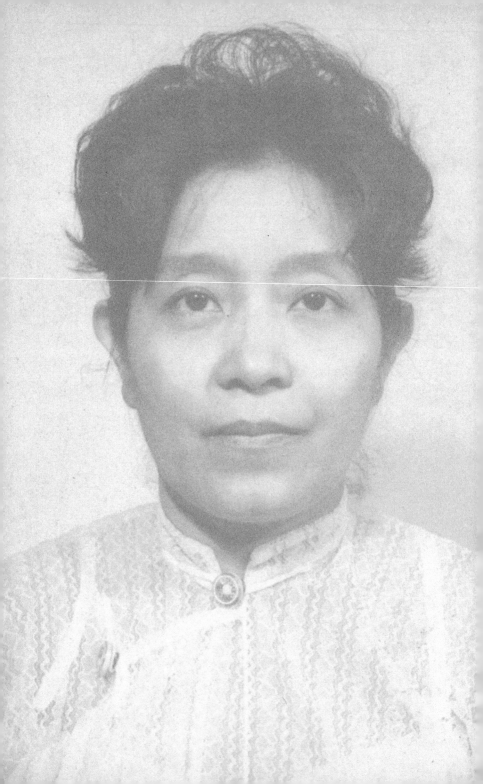

CHAPTER SIXTEEN

As part of my harebrained search for the truth, I decided to ring up the good people at 23andMe for more information, and was eventually put in touch with two company support representatives, Cameron Kruse and Shawna Averbeck.

According to both, there are stages of acceptance that people experience when a DNA test comes back with unexpected results. At first, the science is usually questioned, and according to Kruse, "We explain that we're very confident in the data we return. If someone gets Ashkenazi results, we can fully explain how."

(I *didn't* get Ashkenazi results and wanted to know how this could be, but I'd save that for later.)

Both representatives admitted that the testing process

can make people feel vulnerable and "opened up to the core," but they maintained an upbeat perspective about the results. "As people accept their results and how valid they are—and as they get genetic perspective—they become proud," Kruse declared.

Surely some discoveries were easier to accept as "pluses"—or even worn as symbols of ethnic pride. But what about results that challenged generations of accepted history? Assuming the results were accurate, learning something permanently life-altering about one's people seemed like it would be startling—or even require some support.

How confident were these 23andMe employees in their results? Kruse said that in his line of work, ancestry concerns "ran the gamut," but he said calls about Native American genetics were common and sometimes necessitated certain sleuthing.

"Someone might be confident that they have Native American ancestry—and then the genetic test doesn't reflect that," he explained. "Maybe there were tales in their family history about Native American ancestors, and then [those tales] turned out not to be true."

Kruse was confident that whatever data 23andMe was using behind the scenes to determine this kind of ancestry was the right stuff: "We have a good Native American reference population," he assured me. "If there's a Native

American in there, it should be reflected." (As long as, a company representative later stipulated, the Native American was not "very far back" in the generations.)

I kept hearing about these so-called "reference populations." But what exactly was a "Native American reference population"? I didn't expect that each of these companies had *actual* Native American people in the lab helping to analyze spit samples.

What I did gather from this conversation was that whoever these Native Americans were, 23andMe believed they were definitely getting enough data from them.

Obviously, it wasn't that simple.

Though I had entrusted these companies with my saliva and cheek cells, I had not the faintest clue what they were looking for or how they interpreted their results. I'd blindly assumed science would work it all out and give me the answer, and that the answer would remain uncontested because, hey, it was science.

I decided I would try to figure out what was going on by starting with the type of tests themselves.

Suddenly I remembered that there were references to "Y chromosome" and "mitochondrial DNA" testing on these ancestry websites. I had made my father take one of those Y chromosome tests. I remembered from biology class that men have X and Y chromosomes and women have two X chromosomes—so it turns out that male ancestry is mostly tested via the Y chromosome—which passes down genetic traits from father to son. Okay, I mostly remembered from biology class . . . and then I looked it up on the internet.

Women, meanwhile, are tested using mitochondrial DNA—which reveals genetic traits passed down from mother to daughter in the same way that Y chromosomes reveal genetic clues inherited along the paternal line. (For the record, mothers also pass their mitochondrial DNA to their sons, but those sons can't, in turn, pass it to their children. It travels with moms only.)[1]

In other words, the primary—and most reliable— DNA tests (Y chromosome and mitochondrial DNA) reveal details about either your father's father's line (if you're a man) or your mother's mother's line (if you're a woman). By all accounts, these kinds of tests provide conclusive evidence if you need an answer on something such as paternity or maternal health, or, in my case, your father's father's father's potentially Jewish DNA.

But there are significant blind spots if you use only these two tests. A mitochondrial DNA test will give me reliable information on my mother's mother and her mother and her mother before that. But the further back in generations you go, the bigger an issue this becomes.

Not only will this test leave out all the fathers and grand-fathers from back in the day, it will also leave out any information about the mothers of all those fathers and grandfathers, as well as the fathers and grandfathers of all those mothers. It's almost like an SAT question—and I hated the SATs.

I had to draw a chart to confirm just how many an-cestors this would exempt, and as it turns out, that num-ber doubles with every generation. By the time you got to my great-great-grandparents (the parents of Henry Wagner and U Myint Kaung and Daw Thet Kywe), a mitochondrial DNA test would return information on only one out of sixteen of them.

Like so:

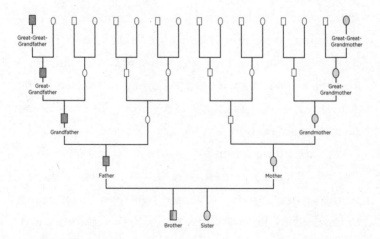

So this was a problem.

Scientists recognize this flaw and in recent years have developed what's known as "autosomal testing." And here's where the story gets really interesting. But first, some background information: Most humans are born with twenty-three pairs of chromosomes. These chromosomes carry the DNA within which the genetic code is written. Autosomal testing scans the genetic material that is found on chromosomes one through twenty-two. (The twenty-third, and last, chromosome is where the X-Y gender stuff is.) There's a ton of DNA material inherited from *both* parents on these chromosomes. That means the process searches for what are known as genetic "markers" of certain ethnic groups.

This is how it works: DNA testing companies take DNA samples from people who belong to "Old World" populations—meaning populations that can be traced back to before the days of cross-culturalism (like, say, an Iroquois population before Europeans arrived in the Americas). These are the "reference populations" I had been so confused about. It's not that actual people are at the lab, sitting around comparing their spit to yours. Instead, scientists and for-profit companies travel the world to find groups of people who have been mostly untouched by genetic "mixing," whether through economic, social, or geographic isolation.

Members of these populations usually have to prove that both of their grandparents have comparable ancestry. With that established, these people are considered to have DNA that is therefore relatively homogenous, or similar. When scientists gather the DNA from the group, it forms what's known as a "reference population" for a specific group of people.

Geneticists scan the reference populations to determine if there are unique DNA markers in each group—and these are known as ancestry-informative markers, or AIMs. These reference populations—basically large(ish) DNA databases—are often then purchased by the big testing companies, including 23andMe, AncestryDNA, and Family Tree DNA. This is what that disclaimer on the 23andMe website was referring to with its warning:

> *This report CANNOT tell you ancestry estimates for populations for which we do not have sufficient data.*

Which raises the question: Okay, which populations have these companies gathered "sufficient data" on?

When people like me want to find out who their ancestors were, our autosomal DNA is scanned for those ancestry-informative markers—the AIMs. Depending on what AIMs come up, scientists make a call about your ancestry. So, for example, if 22 percent of my autosomal DNA shows the AIMs that correspond to the reference population for Northern European, then by that math, I'm 22 percent Northern European.

As you can imagine, there are *a lot* of complications with this process.

First off: Who's to say what "unmixed" or "pure" blood means? The very idea of homogenous, "unmixed" blood is . . . highly questionable. I mean, at what point in history could blood even be considered "pure"? Before East Asian blood mixed with Portuguese blood? Or before East Asian blood mixed with other, *different* East Asian blood? The year 1492 is *one* line you could draw between the Old World and the New, but there are plenty of other moments in history that came before and after that— when populations mixed with one another and the DNA of a people was forever changed. The British colonized Burma in the mid-1800s, but the Pyu of Yunnan entered Lower Burma in 200 BC, and the Mon of Indochina arrived around AD 1000. At what point was Burmese blood considered "unmixed" and free of outside influence? The determination was subjective and largely dependent on what sort of time frame you were looking at: hundreds of years ago . . . or thousands of years ago. Or millennia.

And then there was the issue of the map. Some DNA

was classified using political borders (for example, Irish DNA versus English DNA), while other DNA was defined by region (for example, South Asian DNA). But, I wondered, what countries made up South Asian versus South*east* Asian DNA? Differentiation between the two depended on the borders you drew—and in the nineteenth and twentieth centuries, borders were fairly subjective lines. Remember, if you will, that the Burmese were understood to be part of "British India" while under colonial rule. A paper written several years ago by several leading evolutionary geneticists noted:

> *Many estimations of genetic ancestry are designed to distinguish contributions from reference populations that live in particular geographic regions (e.g., West Africa, Europe, East Asia, and the Americas) that were prominent in colonial-era population movements. This creates a bias that might lead us to define ancestry in reference to particular soci[al] and political groups. Moreover, our knowledge of diversity, and hence the genetic contributions to ancestry, of populations in many other parts of the world (e.g., East Africa, South Asia, Arabian Peninsula, and Southeast Asia) is limited.[2]*

The effects of European colonialism . . . they were inescapable. The Europeans who had invaded countries east and west, from Burma to the United States and everywhere in between, were the ones who shaped how we define a people—to this day! And it was clear that these genetic testing companies held on to these colonial ideas, defining blood and borders on Western, white, European terms.

So scientists were rightfully cautioning that we have been classifying our ancestors using the arbitrary lines drawn in the sand by Europeans over a century ago. But the British and French knew little to nothing about the genetic contributions of the Mon and the Pyu—I mean, they had named the country "Burma" after the Bamah and, in so doing, basically delegitimized the other 135 ethnic groups within the country's borders. Using such outmoded ideas of ethnicity and genetics—in the twenty-first century—seemed questionable and unreliable. I was offended for my Burmese people who would have their lives measured against a British yardstick (once again) or whose biological contributions might not even register.

Even if we could pinpoint some moment in time before which all DNA everywhere was homogenous and afterward was heterogeneous (meaning: mixed)—how to find people who still had that DNA? To find men and women who had lived in geographic isolation for such an extended period of time seemed rather difficult, especially these days.

And then there were those problematic reference populations. How many people were enough to make a "population," anyway? Were the reference populations for the Bamah as sizable as the ones for, say, the Irish? I imagined that consumer tests were in much higher demand among Irish Americans than, say, among the Burmese. Especially because Burma had languished in poverty and an internet blackout for most of the early twenty-first century—the Burmese were (generally) not easily able to drop one hundred bucks for a genetics test they had to order online. If there wasn't a lot of demand coming from Rangoon, then my guess was that the testing companies wouldn't be going out of their way to find Bamah reference populations.

On its website, 23andMe used to provide this information about its DNA database: "We compiled a set of 10,418 people with known ancestry, from within 23andMe and from public sources." Most of the reference data sets, according to the company, come from its consumer database (from DNA that was submitted by people who have purchased the kits). The rest come from public data sets, including the Human Genome Diversity Project, HapMap, and the 1000 Genomes Project. So 23andMe wasn't relying on purchased DNA—it was relying on public databases . . . and on DNA from its users.

But if the bulk of its reference data was coming from the company's users, wouldn't that mean that DNA was mostly from affluent, educated Americans who could afford to drop a hundred bucks on a test—which is to say, mostly white folks?

I got on the phone with 23andMe's senior director of research, Joanna Mountain, and asked her whether the diversity of the data sets was a concern. Mountain explained that the company was working with geneticists elsewhere in the world—in places including Sierra Leone, Congo, and Angola—as part of their "focused efforts to expand the diversity." But these "special collections" of data weren't being used at that time—they were still in the collection phase, according to Mountain. And she didn't have a timeline for when they might be available.

With this in mind, I wondered how big (or small) the reference populations happened to be for each region in my *own* ancestry breakdown. Bear with me for some number-crunching: For my broadly 44 percent "East Asian and Native American" heritage—which comprised Native American (Colombian, Karitiana, Maya, Pima, Surui), East Asian, Japanese, Korean (South Korean), Yakut, Mongolian (Daur, Hezhen, Mongolian,

Oroqen, Tu, Xibo), Chinese (Chinese, Han, Hong Kongese, Taiwanese), and Southeast Asian (Burmese, Cambodian, Indonesian, Lao, Malaysian, Filipino, Thai, Vietnamese) blood—23andMe was using 808 samples from its consumers and 560 from public databases, for a total of 1,368 samples overall.

For my less than .1 percent Sub-Saharan African heritage—West African (Bantu, Cameroonian, Ghanaian, Ivorian, Liberian, Luhya, Mandinka, Nigerian, Sierra Leonean, Yoruba), East African (Eritrean, Ethiopian, Maasai, Somali), Central and South African (Biaka Pygmies, Mbuti Pygmies, San)—the company was using 228 samples from consumer DNA and 393 from public databases, for a total of 621 samples overall.

I asked her how much data was "enough data" to obtain an accurate result, and Mountain offered, "It's not that we say, 'We need a minimum of this.' We look at the data we have and say, 'How granular can we get?'"

In cases where the reference populations are smaller, for example, the "South Asian" population, Andy Kill, another 23andMe employee, explained to me, "That forces us to be more general in the result." He later added, "In cases where we can't pinpoint a certain country, we will up-level that assignment to a region." This is why the company labeled those segments of my DNA "Broadly South Asian," rather than citing specific countries.

On that note, I asked Mountain: How did the company define "countries"—given the fact that a place like Burma, and its borders, had changed mightily over the years? She offered a confusing non-answer. "It's not today, but it is not that far back in time." She added, later, that this meant specifically before people could travel across continents by airplane.

In the months after I spoke to Mountain, 23andMe began offering its users an Ancestry Timeline, which tells you the time period in which you theoretically inherited that French DNA (for me, sometime between 1860 and 1920) or that Chinese DNA (between 1770 and 1860). But that doesn't take into consideration the fact that China in the late eighteenth century looked different on the map from what it does today—it just means that one of my relatives in that time period gave me what we now consider to be "Chinese DNA."

AncestryDNA, meanwhile, informed users that its "reference panel (version 2.0)" contained 3,000 DNA samples from people in twenty-six global regions. This was just a fraction of the data that 23andMe was using. Given that there are over fifty million people in Burma alone—the fact that AncestryDNA had only 3,000 samples spanning less than a seventh of the globe seemed . . . not all that comprehensive.

For the region of "South Asia" (India, Pakistan,

Nepal, Bhutan, Bangladesh, Sri Lanka, and Burma), AncestryDNA had 161 reference samples on file.

For "East Asia" (including Russia, China, North Korea, South Korea, Mongolia, Burma, Japan, Taiwan, Philippines, Indonesia, Thailand, Laos, Cambodia, Vietnam, Singapore, Brunei, and Palau), the company had 645 samples.

For Eastern Europe, it had 646. (To ballpark the ratio here: If you include just Ukraine, Poland, Romania, the Czech Republic, Hungary, Belarus, Bulgaria, Slovakia, and Moldova, then the population of the region would be somewhere around 150 million people.)

I got on the phone with Cathy Ball, Ancestry's chief scientific officer, and again asked what she thought was a "good" amount of data for an accurate reference population. Ball gave me another kind of a non-answer: "You will never get any scientist to say, *I don't need more data*," she said.

I asked her whether certain populations would have more comprehensive reference material because of market demand—testing my theory that there would be more DNA information on the Irish than on the Burmese because DNA testing is likely more popular among the Irish than Burmese.

"Absolutely," she responded. "We ask ourselves, 'What would be informative to most Americans? What, in theory, would be useful?' Western Africa, Europe—those people are places where we concentrate on. England, Ireland, Scotland. Part of it is opportunity. Some places we don't have—and it's basically practicalities. Maybe [samples] weren't collected there and we don't have a ton of customers building family trees [from those places].

"Then there are places like China," she continued, "where you have multiple ethnicities, and it's gonna be pretty hard to know who's Han Chinese and who's from another ethnic group. We don't claim to be specialists, but we try our best.

"And then there are places like Egypt," Ball added, "where people have been going back and forth for years, and what does it mean to be Egyptian? It's messy but it's also interesting."

Indeed, it was interesting, and it was certainly messy. Ball addressed all the concerns I'd had about the accuracy of these tests and confirmed that there *were* reasons to be concerned. There wasn't going to be great reference data for non-western ancestry (like mine—and, oh, billions of other people's). The existing DNA material was often collected and classified according to debatable factors—after all, social, political, and ethnic divisions were not *exactly* standards that everyone agreed upon around the world.

What I was learning in these conversations was that if you were a white person from Europe, you might very well get a more accurate result than, say, if you were a brown person from anywhere else in the world, especially countries without a lot of purchasing power. (What else was new?)

As a case in point: Ancestry had 272 samples on file for Scandinavia (a region of less than 27 million people), but only 161 samples on file for "South Asia" (a region of 1.75 billion people).

Given these statistics, it seemed hard to believe that any of these companies would have enough material to accurately reflect the DNA that might have been carried by my Burmese ancestors in the mid-1800s. This information certainly went a long way in explaining why my mother and grandmother were being assessed with such strong Chinese and Mongolian roots: Those were big parts of the world, and presumably there was more reference data for them.

I wouldn't have been surprised if we were some of the very first Burmese people to even take this test.

CHAPTER SEVENTEEN

I accepted that cultural and genetic borders were never going to be agreed upon, and that each company's DNA database was a work in progress. But the fact that there weren't at least some limitations imposed upon these ancestry results—something beyond the vaguely worded warnings, a clearer signal that the regions and time frames were arbitrary—seemed misleading.

I reached out to the consumer hotline at Family Tree DNA to find out a little more on these ancestry breakdowns and was put in touch with Bennett Greenspan, the company's founder and CEO. I wanted to know if Greenspan had a theory about why I'd been told that I was alternately nearly 15 percent Scandinavian, with little French or German DNA to speak of . . . and also not specifically Scandinavian at all, but instead one-fifth French-German.

At first, Greenspan suggested that one of the tests might be overemphasizing Scandinavian DNA because of the company's database, which had a considerable amount of Scandinavian DNA. If a database, like AncestryDNA, had a particularly large collection of Scandinavian DNA, then, based on logic, it might be more likely to return Scandinavian results for its customers, including me and my father.

But Greenspan's own Family Tree DNA test had returned similar results—in fact, it had shown my father to be 10 percent Scandinavian, while I was allegedly *also* 10 percent Scandinavian. Was this the fault of his database, too? Greenspan was (naturally) more defensive of what his team had determined about my DNA.

"There is some concordance between ourselves and [others]," he offered. "And if you think of your history, those people in Scandinavia came over from places like Poland, Belgium, the Netherlands, and Luxembourg. We're seeing that in your DNA. All of us are kind of a cornucopia of the DNA from the last couple thousand years."

So we were just a cornucopia. Simple as that? Except

for the fact that my father had only *6 percent* Scandinavian DNA, according to Ancestry's test, and I—according to the very same test—had *14 percent* Scandinavian DNA! How was it possible that I—somehow—had more Scandinavian DNA than my father? It was pretty clear that my mother was not Scandinavian.

On this, Greenspan agreed.

"I'm gonna say—and I'm trying to figure out a way to put it nicely—that it's error. It's just noise. It would indicate . . . trying to *overfit* something."

The explanation that being a fifth Scandinavian was "just noise" was a fairly significant concern. It was one thing to be inexact in the art of percentages; it was another when a company was suggesting to a customer that, essentially, her not-so-distant relatives were from Sweden.

Was this sort of ancestral oopsie happening to thousands of other people all over the place? Apparently, this Scandinavian Problem was not limited to just my DNA results: Online amateur genealogists had blogged about their own questionable Scandinavian results.[1] One explanation was that the British Isles were more of a "melting pot" than previously understood, including large populations of Scandinavians who migrated west. If you had Brits in your bloodline, then their DNA might be read as "Scandinavian." Which highlighted the problem I'd had with these classifications all along: At what point did British blood become "British" and at what point was it "Scandinavian"? And, to Cathy Ball's earlier point, wasn't almost all European blood in particular the result of historical mixing? Those darn warring European countries and their intermarriages! Separating that DNA was as arbitrary and confusing as ever.

There seemed to be some agreement about this at least. Joanna Mountain from 23andMe was up-front about the problem. "At times we've over-polled certain ancestries," she admitted.

I couldn't help but think that if some of these companies were making totally inaccurate assumptions about my European heritage, to what lengths were they making errors in areas of the globe where the reference data was even *less* developed? It made me wonder again about my mother's and grandmother's "Mongolian" DNA.

Ball explained one reason why Mongolia often showed up in ancestry reports.

"In China," she said, "it's illegal to collect DNA and take it out of the country, which limits our ability to do those kinds of collections."

Mongolia, Ball explained, "is close to China, so it's

geographically as close as you can get to China without breaking Chinese laws."

In other words, my Burmese DNA *might* have registered as Mostly Chinese (because there was no Burmese DNA on hand), but instead of Mostly Chinese, some of it registered as Somewhat Mongolian (because it was really hard to get Chinese DNA out of China).

Not surprisingly, as it concerned the even smaller and less significant ancestry percentages—my father's .7 percent Balkan bloodline, as reported by 23andMe, for example—certain experts were completely dismissive.

But if a company couldn't come up with one of these alleged and intriguing "really accurate results"—.1 percent Italian, for example—it would be at a market disadvantage. At the same time, it might also be more . . . honest. Slivering DNA slices into tenths of a percent seemed like a fairly exact science. But from what I was seeing, the whole process was supremely *in*exact. These DNA tests claimed that I was a descendant of Genghis Khan and that I was Scandinavian, statements far-fetched enough that they were almost funny. After all this research—all this spitting and cheek-swabbing and questioning of experts (not to mention the money spent)— I was beginning to feel like the entire DNA exercise had been fairly useless.

But Professor Jeffrey Long, professor of evolutionary anthropology at the University of New Mexico, was optimistic about the endeavor. I asked him whether people should believe any of the results they got.

"It depends on the level of precision you want," he told me. "In the broad strokes, people would probably see fairly reasonable results, but oftentimes people aren't interested in the broad strokes. People want to know if they are from a particular locality of the world." People did indeed—even if it didn't matter whether they were actually from that part of the world.

Having spoken to scientists and experts, I came to the conclusion that DNA ancestry testing was a field full of optimism and ambition and broken dreams. It was populated by groups of phonies, pioneers, inventors, enthusiasts, skeptics. Most of the businesses offered the curious customer a chance to learn about their family—an attractive offer—but they were also kind of making promises they couldn't keep.

So why not be more transparent about the shortcuts and standards that were part of the process? Some guidelines were needed to establish how researchers and companies were performing these tests. It seemed to me that guidelines were also needed for how genealogists were determining the ways in which the data was analyzed and interpreted.

I called up Dr. Bamshad, professor of pediatrics and adjunct professor of genome sciences at the University of Washington and a leading authority on evolutionary genetics. He explained that he and some colleagues were trying to establish a way to make the information on reference populations "publicly available and transparent." But not everyone necessarily agreed.

Professor Long said that "the amount of reference data is [much] better" now than it was in the early years of genetic testing. "Some of the companies have very large reference populations," he explained. But he wasn't sure that "it would be possible to [gather] all the reference data available."

If it was too much to hope for more disclosure on company data, what about a window onto the interpretation of the results themselves? After all, the reading of results in an autosomal test is not a 100 percent uncontested science. The tests classify people according to categories that were created, initially, by white Europeans. And then there's the reality that this testing scans only a limited piece of one's genome (i.e., one's complete set of genes)—given how much material there was on chromosomes one through twenty-two.

The American Society of Human Genetics says:

Because the genome is finite, only a small fraction
of ancestors are represented by each given genomic
segment in an individual, and every ancestor does
not necessarily pass on his or her DNA at any given
genomic segment to a descendent, so one can only
ever have limited information on the origins of a
given individual's ancestors.

Shouldn't these companies better explain that the results could be, occasionally, you know, wildly wrong? Only a very small part of the genome is scanned. Those limited results are compared with limited reference data—and *then* assessed according to certain laboratory preferences.

Then again, the different (and sometimes incorrect) results that each company reports is part of what fuels the ancestry market: When one company is able to offer its customers surprising or even shocking genetic information, the pressure is on for all of its competitors to do the same. With "results that make people say, 'I thought I was German, but I'm Scottish!' that's all people want to hear," according to Greenspan.

I confess: For the six days that I believed myself to be partially Scandinavian, I cultivated a taste for free health care and butter cookies, and decided that my

above-average height must be due to my Nordic ancestry. I thought about my Mongolian blood and explained
my love of fur-lined clothing as a taste I'd simply inherited. I felt—fleetingly—a sense of *pride*. A satisfying
peace, as if I could finally say, "Yes, world, this is who I
am: a modern-day mixture of Scandinavian and Mongolian genes, tossed into a blender and thrown halfway
around the world."

But in the end, these percentages, these statistics, were
just a trick. They were brightly colored stones glinting at
the bottom of a riverbed, treats that lured people like me
in by promising one thing and delivering another. Ancestry results played on our most basic desire to know ourselves, to belong to something naturally. And then they
teased that desire by delivering something possibly real,
or possibly watered down with half-truths and educated
guesses.

In the back of my mind, I knew the question of identity and heritage was extremely complicated. It deserved
more care and thoughtfulness than some of these scientists (and myself) might have considered. And so I decided to contact a leading critic of ancestry testing—Troy
Duster, professor of sociology at UC Berkeley. He told
me, "Autosomal AIMs are nutty and complicated, and
that's where the transparency becomes the central issue.

These markers are [developed by companies that] don't want to give away their secrets. . . . If you can't show your strategy . . . then you're asking for a kind of faith on the part of the consumer."

As far as I saw it, Duster hit on the problem with the whole practice of commercial genetics: companies were competing with one another to be the most popular, and also to have the most surprising, exciting results for customers. This was also Greenspan's point. Consumers want accurate results, but they also want some sense of reward, a feeling that they've learned something they didn't know before, that the expensive price tag was worth it. But all of those competing interests can sometimes end in unreliable, inaccurate results.

Was it fair to feel bothered by the fact that most consumers were in the dark about just how much the companies were also in the dark?

I raised this issue with Dr. Long.

"Well," he said, "would you ask for the recipe from the chef if you enjoyed your meal?"

I thought that seemed a silly comparison—after all, I took my spaghetti seriously, but not as seriously as I took my heritage. Dr. Long persisted.

Testing your DNA is like a trip to the fun house, he said. "What if I went to a crystal-ball reader and she told me my sister was not my sister . . . what would I think?

Maybe a reading of your DNA is no more accurate than a crystal ball."

That was a revelation.

"There may not be that much more to the science than crystal-ball reading," Long repeated.

CHAPTER EIGHTEEN

So the DNA tests were compromised, and by "compromised" I mean "possibly inaccurate to the point of being useless." And yet, millions of people were taking them. I tried to sort out what this meant as far as my original questions: Who am I and where do I belong? Was there a solution to the loneliness that had followed me around like a shadow all these years, one that might answer the call for identity and community?

The search for my heritage had changed my understanding of my people. I was not the inheritor of one forgotten society, but, rather, of many Southeastern Asian/ Western European splinter groups: the hustling Luxembourgers, the nationalists of Burma. I was the descendant of a very specific group of (complicated) people.

I was realizing that if, as part of the quest to determine your "identity," you look closely enough at where you come from, you'll inevitably find letdowns, even failures. No one's past is perfect. Instead, if you really examine the branches of your family tree, you'll find that you are a little bit of a lot of things, all mixed together, a person drawn from many different people of many different persuasions. There is resolution in that, but is it the same satisfaction as finally finding your "people"?

Even with the faulty results, the questionable science, and the massive oversimplification of ethnic identity, I had to admit that when I looked at a map of the world highlighting the countries where my DNA could be found, I was awash in pride.

I had no claim to Australia, Greenland, the Middle East, most of East and West Africa, or Russia—but other than those places, the *entire world* was highlighted, blasted into full color by my DNA. This was visual confirmation about the global reach of ol' futureface: I was quite literally a citizen of the world! Here in my body was a real mini–United Nations of genetic material—and that seemed a reason for hope. So much has been made about our borders, how effectively we might close them off and secure the entry points to "protect" our national identity. But here was a body that reached across the world—from sea to shining sea. My DNA map was a rejection of xenophobia, of fear, of superiority. Instead, it was a double-down bet on the world as a sprawling place of communication and comingling.

Would everyone see it this way? Certainly, a good deal of the country is open to the idea of mixing. But not all of it. Specifically: Does America's white majority rejoice at the diversity that lies at the heart of our American heritage—a huge variety of skin colors, beliefs, religions, traditions? A sizable group of white Americans, after all, have made their opinions known—loudly, even violently. They rejected multiculturalism for the familiar terrain of whiteness. They demanded walls and policies to separate, not unite. This America was fearful when it came to other cultures—a fear that was generations old— and the ever-changing and increasingly connected world has done nothing to change that.

Professor Duana Fullwiley at Stanford University, who specializes in medical anthropology, was one of the most prominent voices cautioning against the practice of DNA-based ancestry testing. I asked her whether—in a well-meaning, open-minded quest to erase cultural differences—we might *actually* be unintentionally reinforcing the idea that we were all different from one another, with the DNA percentages a mathematical reminder of those differences.

Professor Fullwiley replied cautiously.

"Well," she said, "it *could* work out that way . . . but I think oftentimes people glom on to two or three specific [parts of their heritage], and these come to represent someone's whole identity. And the methods of these technologies feed that behavior, rather than showing people how [flexible] identity might be. Instead of in[spir]ing people to be more curious about the world, now there are only one or two things they might be focused on."

I asked Professor Fullwiley if she thought DNA testing helped us understand race. She replied: "I don't see [DNA-based ancestry testing] as deconstructing race, as some people do." DNA-based ancestry testing promotes a controversial and basic definition of race, she explained, and often exaggerates the idea of racial differences. "I feel that the tool of ancestry testing, as it's constructed—organized and collected data by continent—reiterates our way of seeing race in simplistic terms."

Many scientists and geneticists agree that the classification of "race" has no basis in scientific reality. In 2000, leaders of the Human Genome Project announced that the human genome contained no real racial differences and that we are all just one race—"the human race."[1] These scientists concluded that human beings share "99.9 percent of their genes, such that researchers cannot point to clear, qualitative genetic breaks between one population and another."[2]

And yet, the practice of DNA detective work emphasizes the opposite. Genetic testing is all about finding *differences* in our genes, not similarities. Fundamentally, these are businesses whose entire model is selling the idea that we are all genetically determined to be different. For example, I am 50 percent European and 37 percent East Asian. As these breakdowns told us, we all had distinct ancestral lines, separate and unique from each other, as determined by a DNA-based test. And where there's difference—no matter how neutral or meaningless—there is an opportunity to turn that difference into someone's favor or fortune.

"The tools we have today that [divide] ancestry in[to] percentages play into the idea that there are pure racial types," Fullwiley told me. The practice of classifying people by their racial makeup, I knew, had sinister echoes throughout history—from pre–Civil War "one-drop" rules (which claimed that anyone with even a single drop of African blood was black and thus less-than) to "racial phrenology," a bogus nineteenth-century non-science that claimed blackness or Jewishness was something to be measured and marginalized (and destroyed, not celebrated).

I recalled an article I'd read earlier by sociologists who were wary about genetic testing and its impact on how we Americans imagine ourselves.

"Websites of many [DNA testing] companies state that race is not genetically determined," the sociologists said, "but the tests nevertheless promote the popular understanding that race is rooted in one's DNA—rather than being an artifact of sampling strategies [and] qualitative boundaries."[3]

Consumers might be led to the iffy conclusion that race was *based* in science. Which it isn't—at least according to most scientists.

"Because race has such profound social, political, and economic consequences," these sociologists concluded, "we should be wary of allowing the concept to be redefined in a way that obscures its historical roots and disconnects it from its cultural and socioeconomic context."[4]

But when I asked evolutionary genetics scholar Dr. Bamshad about how DNA-based ancestry testing was influencing—or perhaps even creating—misguided ideas about race, he agreed that race was "not a very good tool for classifying populations," but he said he did not consider race entirely irrelevant.

"Race is one of many ways to define populations," he explained. "Any definition of a population is relatively gray, because you have to make an arbitrary definition of where to draw the line. There are hundreds of definitions of race. But race captures some biological information: It's one of many identities that a person has. [We see] genetic ancestry and popular notions of race—as well as other parts of identities—as overlapping with one another. They overlap to different extents in different people."

Dr. Bamshad concluded, "Do common notions of race used in the United States capture some information about your biological and genetic identity? Absolutely. In the overwhelming majority of people, that is absolutely true. The better question is: Is that information meaningful? If so, in what context, and in what way?"

For me, it boiled down to one question: Was this stuff moving us closer together or farther apart?

I asked Professor Long, the man who put as much stock in DNA-based ancestry testing as he did in crystal-ball reading.

"Unfortunately," he said, "I think it's moving us toward more division. And this is something that bothers me about the field. As an evolutionary biologist, I have to think of unity and diversity simultaneously."

When you looked at ancestry tests, Long said, "You're looking at the top ten feet of the tree, rather than the whole tree. All my genes are African—but they were given to me by Europeans. That's how I like to think about it. Genetic ancestry has been transferred, but there's no point at which it starts."

I liked this concept. In the beginning, we were all the same; we just took different routes to get to our modern selves. Some people took the Andes, others trekked across sub-Saharan Africa, and still others walked an overland route across the frozen Bering Strait.

Ancestry tracing is a greedy sport: People who do it want as much information and as many statistics as possible. While some people's results confirm the identities they've long held, other results throw these identities into question. And letting go of one's claim to a specific heritage is difficult. Especially in a country with such a deeply personal and political divide over identity.

For his part, the ancestry-testing critic Professor Duster was resolute: ancestry maps—like the one I had gazed on with pride—had negative outcomes. Duster recalled the work of Professor Jennifer Lee at the University of California, Irvine. "What she's shown is how, even though we're all mixed in this way and that, when you have an Asian and white mixture, you still get a binary [or divided] world. You don't have people saying, 'We're mixed!' People identify with one or the other. Asian-white students may get categorized as hapa, but when it comes down to their actual activities, look at the patterns in terms of dating and marriage—and it is dramatic."

I thought about this as it concerned myself, a hapa of Asian-white parentage. And it was mostly true: Growing up, I had identified with white culture (*Saved by the Bell, Garfield*) more than Asian culture (Thingyan celebrations, durian fruits). I married a (really very great) white guy. I attributed this to the fact that I was raised in a very white quadrant of northwest Washington, D.C., and was—in my classes and on my sports teams and in my professional adult life—mostly surrounded by white people.

I was still proud of and excited by my Burmese heritage. In fact, I understood it to be a mark of honor, the thing that made me futureface, the thing that set me apart from . . . all those white people. And by the way, I like to think that if I could have gained entry into a Burmese peer group that wasn't largely composed of bullying twelve-year-old boys throwing water at me in the chilly weeks of early spring, I would have. Maybe I would even have married one.

As I defensively reasoned through all this with myself, I felt a creeping sense of apprehension, because, well, I hadn't really ever looked for that group of friends, nor had I dated that phantom Burmese suitor. I hadn't poked at that other half of me—the Asian side—until recently, when I realized how much of my culture I was in the dark about. Maybe that was the result of circumstances; maybe I lacked curiosity; maybe I was lazy.

Or maybe it was because it was a lot easier to be perceived as white than as Asian where I was growing up, surrounded by the people I was surrounded with, working with the people I came to work with. They were all white! And part of succeeding in their world meant fitting in. And fitting in meant embracing the dominant culture, which was . . . white culture—not someone else's.

Here was a sad truth: being able to throw the signs and read the cues of white people made it easier for me to enter the world of Ivy League universities and American media. I wanted to believe that I could get ahead, no matter what my culture or gender. But I am not sure I could have been as successful in one culture while still being a part of another. Whiteness, even in the twenty-first century, remains a fairly exclusive membership. So along the way, I put aside my Burmeseness. That was just the way it was.

Maybe Duster and Lee were right: Nobody really existed simultaneously in multiple racial worlds, no matter what their ancestry results said. Belonging was still a binary idea—you either belonged or you didn't. And breakdowns of our ancestry might not bring us together any more than hyphenated ethnic designations—African-American, Asian-American, etc.—made society more accepting. People still pick and choose who they are (and who they want to befriend or date), even if the offerings themselves happen to be more diverse. I am a case in point.

Perhaps the only useful truth that had been revealed in all this ancestral investigation is this: we are all from the same place. We took different paths to get here; we made different choices along the way; we checked off different boxes when it came time to decide on language or politics or cuisine or values. And as much as those divergent choices have pushed us apart, placed us lately in different parts of the globe or on opposite sides of a border, the beginning remains immutable, constant, reassuring. It is a reminder that ultimately, we are all in this together—still.

We are, furthermore, in constant motion—this is the course of *Homo sapiens* on planet Earth. In particular, this is what knits Americans together: the fact that a great deal of genetic motion has come to a rest, fairly recently, in this place, on this land.

And that's what my world map of DNA made clear. Alexandra Swe Wagner was (yes) born into somewhat complicated stock, composed of men and women of sometimes contradictory morals. But if I delved further back in time, if I looked at what the map was really telling me, it was that I am a product of people who lived and died far away from the country I call home.

The lesson was not about how my people had assimilated into American culture or their immigrant heroics; it was another thing entirely. The map revealed that my— our—circle of human existence is always widening, and will continue to widen with the passage of time. The genes in my family tree will not be American forever.

Take a look at the Wagner ancestry map in several generations, and I'll bet you the center of action will be in another part of the globe entirely. And this, at last, is the whole point: We come from the same place, and despite our separations over generations, we are ultimately headed back together—in ever-widening circles of travel and marriage and childbirth and time. Genetically speaking, we are one.

Specifically speaking, as it concerns the reason I embarked on this historical/archival/genealogical voyage, the entire concept of "my people" was turning out to be something entirely different from what I had imagined it might be.

So what was the story that I could tell about myself, to myself, to explain who I was?

The story I would tell was straightforward, unfussy: I *was* part of a community. My people weren't dead; they were very much living. They were grappling with change and uncertainty, and looking to do what seemed the most right, as far as they could determine. They didn't necessarily share my genes, or bloodline, or DNA, or even geography. Instead, they were the people, young and old, who struggled in similar ways and held fast to the same ideals and sought good answers to heavy problems. I realized, after all my research was done, after looking so hopefully to the past, that the present was the only community I would and could ever know. The struggles of today, the hope for the future, the examination of the past—these were the foundations of community.

I have recognized my people—fleetingly. They were the ones digging in their pockets for loose change to give to the kid playing the buckets on the subway platform. The ones who gathered together to involve themselves in issues they cared about. The ones who remembered the friend who hadn't been in touch much lately, and *shouldn't we check on him to see if he's doing okay?*

My people were the ones going to the church and the synagogue and the mosque and the monastery, not because they were being forced to or because it was expected, but because the core principles of these faiths—mercy and kindness and goodwill—were things that not only appealed to them, but that they wished to cultivate more specifically in their own lives.

These days, my people are the ones looking at the paper—whether conservative or progressive—furrowing their brows at the headlines, turning up the radio for the story about health care or immigration, hitting send on an email with important political information. They are scared, some of the time, about what lies ahead—but they still believe that if they try hard enough, they might fix it, might steer a more righteous course.

All those years back, I thought I was alone—the only noise in the world was the sound of a shuffling deck of cards, preparing another lonesome game of solitaire. But there was life down the street and up the block, in other rooms, other cities—I just hadn't found it yet, hadn't bought the plane ticket or opened the guidebooks. I was too young!

I'd find it not in Rangoon or Esch, in places my family had long since moved on from, among people who were no longer ours. My blood was not coursing through these lost cities. Instead, it was gushing through New York, where I had made my home and found myself rushing from one chaotic place to the next on crowded subway cars and city sidewalks. Or it was in Mumbai, or Detroit, cities where life was being rebuilt or created anew. Places where movement was constant and change was continual, but optimism was always present—you couldn't survive in these towns without it. My people were the crowds: swarming, moving groups who were white and black and brown. In these sprawling, terrifying metropolises that very nearly ate you up, the process of exploring and connecting would inevitably lead you to the things and people that made it worth staying, made it worth trying to be the best version of yourself you could possibly be.

I had been looking in all the wrong places for the string that connected us—in family lore and foreign cities and dusty files and sampled spit. I had asked men and women from the past for the answers to my questions in the present. Of course they couldn't give them to me, couldn't tell me who I was and where I belonged. The people who knew (even without knowing they knew) were alive. They'd been with me from the beginning.

EPILOGUE: A WORD ABOUT LIVING (AND DYING)

"Alex," my father would say, "we are born alone, and we will die alone," and I would roll my eyes in exaggerated boredom when he said this. But when he did die, unexpectedly, it was indeed alone. Perhaps the only expected part of his sudden death was the fact that it was so singularly lonesome, a fulfillment of the prophecy he'd told me so many times before. His last moments were spent by himself in the house where we'd lived as a family—until divorce and college and adulthood made it so there was no real family unit left to speak of.

The mailman found him, a worker from the same occupation as my father's own father. As far as my father had come—as many miles as he'd put between himself and small-town America and its customs—it was a representative of that world, where things were delivered by hand and neighbors knocked on doors regularly, who ushered him out. As sad as this was, I think it would have made him happy.

In the days after he died, there were phone calls and emails, flowers, a few handwritten notes and text messages, all expressing a certain amount of shock and sadness, but also regret. "We hadn't seen each other in so long!" one said. "I always wondered how he was doing," wrote another. "We'd always ask each other—have you seen Carl?"

It was clear that many people my father had known for the definitive years of his life—which is to say, his life when he lived it largest and most fully—had become, however unintentionally, alienated. My father was proud and angry and could hold a grudge. Even the best of his friends would remark on the explosive nature of their friendship, and he had, especially in his later years, grown more alone.

There were people he saw in passing, of course: neighbors with whom he shared gardening tips or dry cleaners with whom he engaged in casual political talk, a handful of people he'd meet for a drink or for lunch. But his community—the ones who remembered his work at the Democratic National Convention in 1980 or could recall the hotshot organizer from George McGovern's

1972 campaign for president—the friends who had defined his world, who knew him intimately, and who had understood his passions and grievances and inspirations? They had, in many ways, faded into the background.

My father became a source of wistful nostalgia about his old glories, content to reminisce about who he'd been rather than repair the relationships that had made him the man he understood himself to be. He was preoccupied with the past, and struggled to push forward in the present by navigating the necessary ups and downs of life and love. While this may have been an easier way to live, it was also a lot lonelier.

His life had become disconnected from the here and now. He, like so many others, had shied away from the often complex reality of who we are for, instead, the myth of who we once were. And his death marked an endpoint not simply to his life, but to the honey-hued family narrative about Iowa corncobs and stickball at sunset, the frozen Mississippi in winter and the decency of the lone black dry cleaner in town.

This was the end of the fable about our people. Now, I knew a more authentic, though less tidy, family history that was equal parts comedy and tragedy. I could tell my son about his grandfather and his great-grandfather. What made them compelling and what mistakes they'd made along the way. What was gained and what was lost.

Where we had come from—and who had been there be-fore. What we earned and what we were given. Here was a chance to open a new chapter, this time with the truth. To live in the world—as difficult and complex and heart-breaking as it can be—and not in the past.

The other side of my family tree had grown more complicated as well. I had started this fantastic adventure by speaking with the oldest person I knew, Mya Mya Gyi. She was in her late nineties, and it was a race against time to get as much information from her as possible. With her, I could feel the sands slipping through the hourglass, the seconds ticking away on the clock. Sometimes I even panicked. Who else would have the information she had? Who would remember the things she did about our fam-ily? About Burma? Where else could I learn about un-resolved conflicts of our people? Time was running out, and there was so much more to know! It was stressful.

Each time we spoke, I was struck by how much you could pack into nine decades of life. How if you were curious and brave, your time on earth would seem very long indeed. How high the highs of a life well lived, how deep the lows of unresolved mistakes! She'd seen so much of this world, met so many people; all the diamonds and curries and bowls of piping hot chicken noodle soup she'd had since that very first one, during her first winter in America. She lived in worlds upon worlds, ones that kept unfolding with each stage of her life. What a seemingly unstoppable life she had lived.

Near the end of my research, my grandmother fell sick abruptly. This was not the first time she had battled illness, of course—I figured she'd survived so much that she would certainly survive this sickness, whatever it was. Because of course she would. She was unstoppable. But no, this time she did not. She grew very weak and stopped opening her eyes to us, and no amount of chicken broth would pass her lips.

Her last words were not to me, or my mother, or any number of relatives who stopped by to pay their respects and say goodbye. Instead, her last comments in this life were to my husband, who stopped in her room late one afternoon and happened to be wearing a brand-new watch. He appeared in the doorway, and, sensing his presence, she opened her eyes and said, "Good to see you!" as if it were teatime and she wasn't on her deathbed. He came closer to her and, without looking down, she said to him—the last thing Mya Mya the Emerald would ever say—"Nice watch."

Of course, we all laughed. None of us could believe that in the end, this is what she left us with. But to her, having closure, or some sort of meaningful goodbye, was beside the point. This is what I realized only after the fact, when this whole project was completed: She wasn't thinking of last rites or leaving us with some Epic Final Thought, because for her, there was no last of anything. There was no reliance on dim memories: There was only the making of new ones. And all this, her Buddhism taught, would continue—until nirvana had been reached.

I wasn't a devout Buddhist, but I, too, had come to the realization that our story—which was necessarily her story—continued. My grandmother didn't need to say something definitive or profound to me the day she died, because it wasn't the final word on anything. She may have been done on this earthly world, but her children and her children's children (and their children!) were still alive. She wouldn't know where we ended up or how the story changed, what twists and turns awaited her family— but she wasn't worried.

It was up to us.

ACKNOWLEDGMENTS

Thank you to:

First and foremost, Chris Jackson, who worked with me on this project for many too many years, and who made a confusing jumble of thoughts into an actual book with purpose. The thing you are holding in your hand would not exist without him (I really mean this).

Eli Horowitz, for being patient and thoughtful, as he always is, and for helping me channel the necessary Muse of Mystery required to write a book of this sort.

Cousin Geoff Aung, for indulging the harebrained spirit of this endeavor and helping with all manner of Burma research and obscure Burma political history.

Cousin Karl Wagner, for planting the seed of curiosity and helping to make it grow.

My mother, Swe Thant, for answering too many questions and having an extraordinary generosity of spirit when it came to the ambitions of this book.

And thank you to my husband, Sam Kass, who is my lighthouse—and without whom I would be lost. What luck that I get to live this life with you.

NOTES

CHAPTER ONE

1. "The New Face of America," *Time,* special issue, November 18, 1993, cover, content.time.com/time/covers/0,16641,19931118,00.html.

CHAPTER TWO

1. Gregory Rodriguez, "How Genealogy Became Almost as Popular as Porn," *Time,* May 30, 2014, time.com/133811/how-genealogy-became-almost-as-popular-as-porn.

CHAPTER FOUR

1. Adrian Levy and Cathy Scott-Clark, "Between Hell and the Stone of Heaven," *The Observer,* November 10, 2001, www.theguardian.com/theobserver/2001/nov/11/features.magazine37.
2. Sean Turnell, "Cooperative Credit in British Burma" (IDEAS Working Paper Series from RePEc, 2005), 5.
3. S. D. Sharma, ed., *Rice: Origin, Antiquity, and History* (Enfield, N.H.: Science Publishers, 2010), 459.

4. U Khin Win, *A Century of Rice Improvement in Burma,*
   International Rice Research Institute (Los Baños,
   Philippines, 1991).
5. John F. Cady, *A History of Modern Burma* (Ithaca:
   Cornell University Press, 1958), 72–73.
6. Bureau of International Labor Affairs, "Child Labor
   and Forced Labor Reports: Burma," 2016, www.dol
   .gov/agencies/ilab/resources/reports/child-labor
   /burma.
7. Turnell, "Cooperative Credit in British Burma," 17.
8. Government of Burma, *Report of the Land and
   Agriculture Committee, Part III: Agricultural Finance;
   Colonisation; Land Purchase* (Rangoon: Superintendent
   of Government Printing, 1938), 90.
9. Government of Burma, *Report of the Burma Provincial
   Banking Enquiry Committee, 1929–30: Volume I*
   (Rangoon: Superintendent of Government Printing,
   1930), 176.
10. Nalini Ranjan Chakravarti, *The Indian Minority in
    Burma* (London: Oxford University Press for the
    Institute of Race Relations, 1971), 28.

CHAPTER FIVE

1. Hans-Bernd Zöllner, ed., Myanmar Literature Project,
   Working Paper No. 10:12, "Material on Thein
   Pe: Indo-Burman Conflict," www.phil.uni-passau

.de/fileadmin/dokumente/lehrstuehle/korff/pdf
/research/mlp12.pdf.

2. Donald M. Seekins, *State and Society in Modern Rangoon* (London: Routledge, 2011), 44.

3. Zöllner, "Material on Thein Pe: Indo-Burman Conflict," 133.

4. Donald Eugene Smith, *Religion and Politics in Burma* (Princeton: Princeton University Press, 1965), 109–10. Also see Michael Adas, *The Burma Delta: Economic Development and Social Change on an Asian Rice Frontier, 1852–1941* (Madison: University of Wisconsin Press, 2011), 206.

5. Chakravarti, *The Indian Minority in Burma,* 158.

6. Chakravarti, *The Indian Minority in Burma,* 158.

7. Kate Hodal, "Buddhist Monk Uses Racism and Rumours to Spread Hatred in Burma," *The Guardian,* April 18, 2013, www.theguardian.com/world/2013 /apr/18/buddhist-monk-spreads-hatred-burma.

8. Krishnadev Calamur, "The Misunderstood Roots of Burma's Rohingya Crisis," *The Atlantic,* September 25, 2017, www.theatlantic.com/international/ archive/2017/09/rohingyas-burma/540513/.

9. "UN Human Rights Chief Points to 'Textbook Example of Ethnic Cleansing' in Myanmar," UN News Centre, September 11, 2017, www.un.org/apps/news /story.asp?NewsID=57490#.WcvzChNSzXQ.

10. Max Bearak, "One Month On, a Bleak New Reality Emerges for 436,000 Rohingya Refugees," *Washington Post,* September 25, 2017.

CHAPTER EIGHT

1. Benjamin Gue, *The History of Iowa* (New York: Century History, 1903).
2. Wikipedia, s.v. "Treaty of Prairie du Chien," last modified May 9, 2017, 19:19, en.wikipedia.org/wiki /Treaty_of_Prairie_du_Chien.
3. Wikipedia, s.v. "Third Treaty of Prairie du Chien," en.wikipedia.org/wiki/Third_Treaty_of_Prairie_du _Chien.
4. Andrew Jackson, *The Papers of Andrew Jackson: Volume VII, 1829,* ed. Daniel Feller, Harold D. Moser, Laura-Eve Moss, and Thomas Coens (Knoxville: University of Tennessee Press, 2007), 541.
5. A. R. Fulton, *The Red Men of Iowa* (Des Moines: Mills & Co., 1882), 148.
6. "Fort Atkinson and the Winnebago Occupation of Iowa, 1840–1849," University of Iowa Office of the State Archaeologist, archaeology.uiowa.edu/sites /archaeology.uiowa.edu/files/FtAtkinson9.pdf.
7. Fulton, *The Red Men of Iowa,* 150.
8. Todd Arrington, "Exodusters," National Park Service

online, www.nps.gov/home/learn/historyculture
/exodusters.htm.

CHAPTER NINE

1. FamilySearch.org Wiki, "United States Naturalization and Citizenship," familysearch.org/wiki/en/United _States_Naturalization_and_Citizenship.

CHAPTER TWELVE

1. Myo Myint, *The Politics of Survival in Burma: Diplomacy and Statecraft in the Reign of King Mindon, 1853–1878* (Ithaca: Cornell University Southeast Asia Program, 1987), 210.
2. James Stuart Olson and Robert Shadle, eds., *Historical Dictionary of the British Empire* (Westport, Conn.: Greenwood, 1996), 2:1088.
3. David Joel Steinberg, ed., *In Search of Southeast Asia: A Modern History* (New York: Praeger, 1971).
4. William J. Topich and Keith A. Leitich, *The History of Myanmar* (Santa Barbara, Calif.: Greenwood, 2013), 48.

CHAPTER THIRTEEN

1. Andrew Pollack, "23andMe Will Resume Giving Users Health Data," *New York Times,* October 21, 2015, www.nytimes.com/2015/10/21/business/23andme

-will-resume-giving-users-health-data.html. Also
see Anne Wojcicki, "A Note to Our Customers
Regarding the FDA," 23andMe blog, February 19,
2015, blog.23andme.com/news/a-note-to-our
-customers-regarding-the-fda, and FDA News Release,
"FDA Permits Marketing of First Direct-to-Consumer
Genetic Carrier Test for Bloom Syndrome," U.S. Food
and Drug Administration, February 19, 2015, www
.fda.gov/newsevents/newsroom/pressannouncements
/ucm435003.htm.

CHAPTER SIXTEEN

1. Steph Yin, "Why Do We Inherit Mitochondrial
   DNA Only from Our Mothers?," *New York Times*,
   June 23, 2016, www.nytimes.com/2016/06/24
   /science/mitochondrial-dna-mothers.html.
2. Charmaine D. Royal, et al., "Inferring Genetic
   Ancestry: Opportunities, Challenges, and
   Implications," *American Journal of Human Genetics* 86(5)
   (2010): 661–73, www.ncbi.nlm.nih.gov/pmc/articles
   /PMC2869013.

CHAPTER SEVENTEEN

1. CeCe Moore, "My Review of AncestryDNA's
   Admixture Tool and a Glimpse into the Future
   of Genetic Genealogy," June 26, 2012, www

.yourgeneticgenealogist.com/2012/06/my-review-of
-ancestrydnas-admixture.html.

CHAPTER EIGHTEEN

1. "Remarks by the President, Prime Minister Tony Blair of England (via satellite), Dr. Francis Collins, Director of the National Human Genome Research Institute, and Dr. Craig Venter, President and Chief Scientific Officer, Celera Genomics Corporation, on the Completion of the First Survey of the Entire Human Genome Project," White House press release, June 26, 2000, www.genome.gov/10001356/june-2000 -white-house-event. Also see Duana Fullwiley, "The 'Contemporary Synthesis': When Politically Inclusive Genomic Science Relies on Biological Notions of Race," *Isis* 105, no. 4 (December 2014): 803–14, www .journals.uchicago.edu/doi/10.1086/679427.

2. Ruha Benjamin, "A Lab of Their Own: Genomic Sovereignty as Postcolonial Science Policy," *Policy and Society* 28(2009): 341–55.

3. Deborah Bolnick, et al., "The Science and Business of Genetic Ancestry Testing," *Science,* April 25, 2011, 399–400.

4. Deborah Bolnick, et al., "The Science and Business of Genetic Ancestry Testing," *Science,* April 25, 2011, 399–400.

ABOUT THE AUTHOR

ALEX WAGNER is a cohost and executive producer of Showtime's political documentary series *The Circus* and a national correspondent for CBS News. She is also a contributing editor at *The Atlantic* and the host of their popular podcast, Radio Atlantic. She was the host of MSNBC's Emmy-nominated *NOW with Alex Wagner.*